HBR's 10 Must Reads

2026

HBR's 10 Must Reads

HBR's 10 Must Reads are definitive collections of classic ideas, practical advice, and essential thinking from the pages of *Harvard Business Review*. Exploring topics like disruptive innovation, emotional intelligence, and new technology in our ever-evolving world, these books empower any leader to make bold decisions and inspire others.

TITLES INCLUDE:

HBR's 10 Must Reads for New Managers
HBR's 10 Must Reads on AI
HBR's 10 Must Reads on Building a Great Culture
HBR's 10 Must Reads on Change Management
HBR's 10 Must Reads on Communication
HBR's 10 Must Reads on Data Strategy
HBR's 10 Must Reads on Decision-Making
HBR's 10 Must Reads on Design Thinking
HBR's 10 Must Reads on Digital Transformation
HBR's 10 Must Reads on Emotional Intelligence
HBR's 10 Must Reads on High Performance
HBR's 10 Must Reads on Innovation
HBR's 10 Must Reads on Leadership
HBR's 10 Must Reads on Leading Winning Teams
HBR's 10 Must Reads on Managing People
HBR's 10 Must Reads on Managing Yourself
HBR's 10 Must Reads on Marketing
HBR's 10 Must Reads on Mental Toughness
HBR's 10 Must Reads on Strategy
HBR's 10 Must Reads on Women and Leadership
HBR's 10 Must Reads Boxed Set (6 Books)
HBR's 10 Must Reads Ultimate Boxed Set (14 Books)

For a full list, visit hbr.org/mustreads.

HBR's 10 Must Reads

2026

Harvard Business Review Press
Boston, Massachusetts

Copyright 2026 Harvard Business School Publishing Corporation

Printed in the United States of America

10 9 8 7 6 5 4 3 2 1

The web addresses referenced in this book were live and correct at the time of the book's publication but may be subject to change.

Cataloging-in-Publication data is forthcoming.

ISBN: 979-8-89279-194-6
eISBN: 979-8-89279-195-3

The paper used in this publication meets the requirements of the American National Standard for Permanence of Paper for Publications and Documents in Libraries and Archives Z39.48-1992.

Contents

Editors' Note

You may notice this year's Must Reads looks a little different—and the changes go deeper than the cover. It still gives you 10 definitive articles, carefully selected by a team of editors. And it still includes a variety of trusted voices—experts, researchers, practitioners, and consultants—discussing some of the most relevant and complex topics in business today. But a lot has changed since we launched these books over a decade ago. And with so many strong ideas now appearing on hbr.org, we decided to include some of these shorter pieces. The "Quick Reads," as we call them, are just as valuable as our longer articles. They have resonated with our readers, and their inclusion provides a fuller picture of how *Harvard Business Review* is tackling today's urgent challenges.

In a year that held a disheartening amount of upheaval—large-scale environmental disasters, layoffs and tightened budgets, and geopolitical conflict—leaders are looking for the best advice on how to move forward more confidently. This year's slate of articles offers just that, drawing insights from some surprising places. You'll read about macroeconomic shocks and Taylor Swift's meteoric rise—and learn from both. You will face the fear your employees feel about AI and automation and unpick the complexities of strategy and culture. This year's lineup will help you navigate the uncertainty and stressors of our world and move toward a more promising future.

We encourage you to truly engage with the content you read here. That's why we've also included a new feature in this volume:

a Discussion Guide with questions you can ask your team, peers, or colleagues about key ideas. Whether you're running a formal book club or just want to have a thoughtful conversation, you can use the guide to take a deeper dive into the articles so you can better digest and apply what you've read.

It's in the spirit of inquiry that we begin the volume. **"The Art of Asking Smarter Questions"** proposes a new approach to your leadership: Stop offering solutions and start asking more questions. While leaders have embraced the importance of curiosity, listening, learning, and humility, they're still fuzzy about the best questions to ask in a given situation. IMD professors Arnaud Chevallier, Frédéric Dalsace, and Jean-Louis Barsoux describe five types of questions you can use in your strategic decision-making and provide a tool to help you assess your interrogatory style.

What kinds of questions do you ask when faced with a first-of-its-kind project? After all, you have nothing to compare it to. That's a common misconception, argue Bent Flyvbjerg, Alexander Budzier, M.D. Christodoulou, and M. Zottoli, all of the University of Oxford and Saïd Business School, in **"The Uniqueness Trap."** Their research shows that the more you think of your project as unique, the more likely you are to underestimate risk, make poor decisions, and blow through budgets and schedules. Instead, they argue, always assume that someone, somewhere has undertaken a project like yours—even if they're in an unrelated industry. Using examples such as decommissioning nuclear power plants in Sweden and building a high-speed rail line in California, the authors show you how to get out of this biased way of thinking and achieve better results.

Many businesses have diverse portfolios. The Clorox Company, for instance, makes branded products ranging from bleach to salad dressing to charcoal. And Berkshire Partners' private equity businesses include fitness platforms, wireless towers, and car wash systems. But corporations often focus more on the makeup of their portfolios than on how to bring value to them. That's a strategic mistake, argue Harvard Business School professors Bharat N. Anand and David J. Collis in **"Why Multibusiness Strategies Fail and How to Make Them Succeed."** "A corporation's scope determines its strategic potential," they write, "but aligning its structure and management processes with its chosen sources of value creation determines the success of its execution." Using the authors' strategy continuum, enterprises can assess where they fall and how their businesses are related to one another. The authors then explain how organizations can align their portfolio selection, structure, and processes with their vision of how to add value.

Whether you lead a multibusiness enterprise with thousands of employees or a small startup with only a handful, you have probably been debating the future of remote work. Return-to-office mandates have been making headlines, but with no real data to back up decisions, it's hard to make the right choice for your business. Fortunately, professors Nicholas Bloom and Ruobing Han and Trip.com Group cofounder and executive chairman James Liang changed that. They ran a six-month experiment to understand the benefits of hybrid work. See what they discovered in their Quick Read article, **"One Company A/B Tested Hybrid Work. Here's What It Found."**

If culture eats strategy for breakfast, how should you be cooking it? In **"Build a Corporate Culture That Works,"** INSEAD professor Erin Meyer notes that organizations often struggle to create cultures that shape the behavior of their employees. All too often a company's culture is described in a way that fails to offer guidance when difficult situations arise. The result is a mismatch between what is *said* to be an organization's culture and what its people actually do. To build a better culture, the author says, leaders should follow six rules: Ground it in the dilemmas you are likely to confront, dilemma-test your values, communicate your values in colorful terms, hire people who fit, let culture drive strategy, and know when to pull back from a value statement.

With so many challenges to focus on—projects, strategy, culture—leaders often miss a critical issue right in front of them: an ineffective executive team. In **"Why Leadership Teams Fail,"** Thomas Keil and Marianna Zangrillo, the authors of *The Next Board*, identify three main patterns of dysfunction in senior leadership teams. Behaviors stemming from these patterns include infighting and political maneuvering; conflict avoidance and an overemphasis on collaboration; and complacency, lack of competence, and an unhealthy focus on past success. The authors then provide practical advice leaders can use to reverse course, eliminate disruptive dynamics, and create a cohesive team at the top.

Companies are wise to prepare for the unpredictable. But how can they judge which risks are genuine? In the past five years, leaders have dealt with a rapid succession of shocks, crises—and false alarms. In **"How to Assess True Macroeconomic Risk,"** Philipp Carlsson-Szlezak and Paul Swartz, both of Boston Consulting Group, argue that leaders should follow three principles: avoid leaning too heavily on any one economic model, ignore the doomsayers in the financial press, and cultivate rational optimism. Doing so will help them to reclaim their own judgment and achieve a true assessment of macroeconomic risk.

In an ideal world, managers would instinctively and unquestioningly champion your efforts. But in reality, your supervisor is busy juggling multiple priorities, and your project may not be top of mind. Many leaders simply don't recognize when their advocacy is needed. In the Quick Read article **"Five Ways to Ask Your Boss to Advocate for You,"** executive coach Melody Wilding offers practical advice on how to approach your manager with such requests—and how to make it equally appealing for them. Learning this skill will help you achieve success not only in your projects but in your career.

The political backlash against diversity, equity, and inclusion programs has left many organizations confused about how—and whether—to continue them. Moreover, many DEI proponents agree that common DEI approaches aren't producing the desired results. In **"What Comes After DEI"** strategist and consultant Lily Zheng suggests another option: the FAIR framework. By emphasizing *fairness* in policies, broad *accessibility*, *inclusive* cultures, and trust-based *representation*, organizations can better address the needs of all employees and create meaningful, lasting change.

Inclusion of another kind is at the heart of our next piece, **"For Success with AI, Bring Everyone On Board."** As advanced technologies assume a larger role in organizations, employees are intimidated. Not only do they worry that AI will take away parts of their jobs, but they also feel excluded from the conversation, unable to offer feedback about what's being done to their roles. David De Cremer, author of *The AI-Savvy Leader*, suggests that to make your AI efforts truly successful, you should involve everyone in your company, from top leadership all the way down. Companies that do so will be more likely to improve long-term performance—and to keep their employees happy, productive, and engaged.

Innovation is all about creating new opportunities to grow, but in **"Design Products That Won't Become Obsolete,"** authors

Vijay Govindarajan, Tojin T. Eapen, and Daniel J. Finkenstadt suggest going a step further: create products that can grow *with* your customers. Using the examples of Radio Flyer's Grow with Me Racer, Keurig K-Duo coffee makers, Because International's Shoe That Grows, and more, they outline the consumer challenges these types of products address, describe how companies use software and hardware to build them, and suggest models for capturing value with them. Companies that shift from offering static offerings to products that can meet the changing preferences of customers will be positioned for success.

The final piece in this volume may surprise you. Instead of focusing on a leading company or an industry titan, we zoom in on a pop star in **"The Strategic Genius of Taylor Swift."** *Harvard Business Review* editor Kevin Evers spent years studying the ins and outs of Swift's career choices and exploring how they map to key concepts in business, from identifying blue oceans in the country music scene to adapting to the shift from radio play to streaming platforms. Whether or not you're a "Swiftie," you'll learn something from her strategic decisions that you can apply to your own work.

The world continues to move quickly and unpredictably, but let the ideas here be your guide, leading you to lessons where you thought there were none—by asking questions, looking to other industries, and even second-guessing what popular news headlines might be telling you. We hope that by reading these articles, you gain confidence in your decision-making and feel better prepared to forge ahead.

—The Editors

HBR's 10 Must Reads

2026

1

The Art of Asking Smarter Questions

by Arnaud Chevallier, Frédéric Dalsace and Jean-Louis Barsoux

As a cofounder and the CEO of the U.S. chipmaker Nvidia, Jensen Huang operates in a high-velocity industry requiring agile, innovative thinking. Reflecting on how his leadership style has evolved, he told the *New York Times*, "I probably give fewer answers and I ask a lot more questions. . . . It's almost possible now for me to go through a day and do nothing but ask questions." He continued, "Through probing, I help [my management team] . . . explore ideas that they didn't realize needed to be explored."

The urgency and unpredictability long faced by tech companies have spread to more-mature sectors, elevating inquiry as an essential skill. Advances in AI have caused a seismic shift from a world in which answers were crucial to one in which questions are. The big differentiator is no longer access to information but the ability to craft smart prompts. "As a leader, you don't have the answers; your workforce [does], your people [do]," Jane Fraser, Citi's CEO, told *Fortune* magazine. "That's completely changed how you have to lead an organization. You have to unleash the creativity. . . . The innovation isn't happening because there's a genius at the top of the company that's coming up with the answers for everything."

Indeed, leaders have embraced the importance of listening, curiosity, learning, and humility—qualities critical to skillful interrogation. "Question-storming"—brainstorming for questions rather than answers—is now a creativity technique. But unlike lawyers, doctors, and psychologists, business leaders aren't formally trained on what kinds of questions to ask. They must learn as they go. (See "The Surprising Power of Questions," HBR, May–June 2018, among others.)

It's not a matter of asking lots of questions in hopes of eventually hitting on the right ones. Corinne Dauger, a former VP of creative development at Hermès, told us, "In a one-hour meeting, there are only so many questions you can ask. . . . So where do you want to spend the time? When you're asking one question, you're not asking another." If any one line of questioning dominates, it inevitably crowds out others. Leaders must also watch for complacency, diminishing returns, avoidance of sensitive topics, and stubbornness.

In our research and consulting over the past decade, we've seen that certain kinds of questions have gained resonance across the business world. And in a three-year project we asked executives to question-storm about the decisions they've faced and the kinds of inquiry they've pursued. In this article we share what we've learned. We offer a practical framework for the types of questions to ask in strategic decision-making and a tool to help you assess your interrogatory style.

Idea in Brief

The Situation

With organizations of all sorts facing increased urgency and uncertainty, the ability to ask smart questions has become key. But business professionals aren't formally trained in that skill.

Why It's So Challenging

Managers' expertise often blinds them to new ideas. And the flow of questions can be hard to process in real time, so certain concerns and insights may never be raised.

The Remedy

Strategic questions can be grouped into five domains: investigative, speculative, productive, interpretive, and subjective. By attending to each, leaders and teams are more likely to cover all the areas that need to be explored—and they'll surface information and options they might otherwise have missed.

The Great Unasked Questions

Before we lay out our framework, we want to emphasize one point above all: The questions that get leaders and teams into trouble are often the ones they fail to ask. These are questions that don't come spontaneously; they require prompting and conscious effort. They may run counter to your and your team's individual or collective habits, preoccupations, and patterns of interaction.

The late scholar and business thinker Sumantra Ghoshal once said that leadership means making happen what otherwise would not. In the realm of inquiry a leader's job is to flush out information, insights, and alternatives, unearthing critical questions the team has overlooked. You don't need to come up with the missing questions yourself, but you do need to draw attention to neglected spheres of inquiry so that others can raise them.

All this is harder than it may sound, for two reasons. First, you may be hampered by your expertise. Your professional successes and deep experience may have skewed your approach to problem-solving. (See "Don't Be Blinded by Your Own Expertise," HBR, May–June 2019.) It can be hard to escape the gravitational pull of such conditioning unless you take a hard look at your question habits. Second, the flow and diversity of questions can be hard to process in real time, especially amid heated exchanges. Often it's only after the fact that you realize certain concerns or options were never raised.

Our research reveals that strategic questions can be grouped into five domains: *investigative, speculative, productive, interpretive,* and *subjective.* Each unlocks a different aspect of the decision-making process. Together they can help you tackle key issues that are all too easy to miss.

Investigative: What's Known?

When they are facing a problem or an opportunity, effective decision-makers start by clarifying their purpose—asking themselves what they want to achieve and what they need to learn to do so. The process can be fueled by using successive "Why?" questions, as in the "five whys" sequence devised by managers at Toyota. Successively asking "How?" can also help you transcend generic solutions and develop more sophisticated alternatives. Investigative questions dig ever deeper to generate nonobvious information. The most common mistake is failing to go deep enough.

It sounds like a straightforward process, but lapses are surprisingly common. In 2014 a failure of investigation led a team at the French rail operator SNCF to neglect an essential piece of data during its €15 billion purchase of 1,860 regional trains. No one thought to ask whether the platform measurements were universal. They weren't. The trains proved too wide for 1,300 older stations—a mistake that cost €50 million to fix. The Spanish train operator Renfe discovered a similar oversight in 2021: The 31 state-of-the-art commuter trains it had ordered were too big to pass through some tunnels in the mountainous areas they were meant to serve. The problem was detected before the trains were built, but delivery was significantly delayed.

Speculative: What If?

Whereas investigative questions help you identify and analyze a problem in depth, speculative questions help you consider it more broadly. To reframe the problem or explore more creative solutions, leaders must ask things like "What if . . . ?" and "What else . . . ?" The global design company IDEO popularized this approach. It systematically uses the prompt "How might we . . . ?"—coined by Min Basadur when he was a young manager at P&G—to overcome limiting assumptions and jumpstart creative problem-solving.

Consider how Emirates Team New Zealand's innovative catamaran won international sport's oldest extant trophy, the America's Cup, in 2017. Crew members pedaled stationary bikes to generate power for the vessel's hydraulic systems rather than turning handles, as was customary. Many observers assumed that the breakthrough question had been "What if we used leg power instead of arm power?" That wasn't a new suggestion, however. Other competitors had considered and rejected the idea, unwilling to hamper crew members' ability to move around the boat. One team had even tried it.

The team from New Zealand went a step further, asking, "What else could a pedal system allow?" It could free up crew members' hands, the team realized, and the boat's hydraulic systems could then be operated with handlebar controls. That distributed the crew's roles more evenly and allowed multiple maneuvers to be executed quickly. The boat could be sailed more precisely and aggressively, leading to an upset win over Oracle Team USA.

Productive: Now What?

Productive questions help you assess the availability of talent, capabilities, time, and other resources. They influence the speed of decision-making, the introduction of initiatives, and the pace of growth.

In the 1990s the CEO of AlliedSignal, Larry Bossidy, famously integrated a focus on execution into his company's culture. He insisted on rigorously questioning and rethinking the various hows of executing on strategy: "How can we get it done?" "How will we synchronize our actions?" "How will we measure progress?" and so on. Such questions can help you identify key metrics and milestones—along with possible bottlenecks—to align your people and projects and keep your plans on track. They will expose risks, including strains on the organization's capacity.

The top team at Lego neglected productive questions when responding to the rise of digital toys in the early 2000s. The toymaker tried to diversify its way out of trouble, introducing several products in rapid succession. The initiatives themselves weren't necessarily misguided, but each meant a stretch into an adjacent area, such as software (Lego Movie Maker), learning concepts (Lego Education), or clothing (Lego Wear). Collectively they far exceeded the company's bandwidth, and Lego suffered record losses in 2003. The following year the incoming CEO, Jørgen Vig Knudstorp, shared his diagnosis of the problem with the board: "Rather than doing one adjacency every three to five years, we did three to five adjacencies every year." He later told the MIT professor David Robertson, "Suddenly we had to manage a lot of businesses that we just didn't understand. We didn't have the capabilities, and we couldn't keep up the pace."

Interpretive: So, What . . . ?

Interpretive questions—sensemaking questions—enable synthesis. They push you to continually redefine the core issue—to go beneath the surface and ask, "What is this problem really about?" Natural follow-ups to investigative, speculative, and productive questions, interpretive questions draw out the implications of an observation or an idea. After an investigative question, you might ask, "So, what happens if this trend continues?" After a speculative question, "So, what opportunities does that idea open up?" After a productive question, "So, what does that imply for scaling up or sequencing?"

Interpretive questions come in other forms, too: "What did we learn from this?" "How is that useful?" "Are these the right questions to ask?" In an interview on *The Tim Ferriss Show,* Daniel Ek reflected on what he considered his chief role as the CEO of Spotify: "It's almost always back to purpose—like, Why are we doing things? Why does it matter? How does this ladder up to the mission?"

A decision-making process should always circle back to interpretive questions. They provide the momentum to move from one mode of inquiry to another, and they convert information into actionable insight. Even solid analyses are ineffectual if you fail to make sense of them. Ten years ago we worked with the top team at a high-end European car manufacturer. When we brought up Tesla's recently released all-electric sedan, some of the engineers laughed. "There's a seven-millimeter gap between the door and the chassis," one said. "These people don't know how to make a car."

That was a serious error of sensemaking. By focusing on a technical imperfection, the automaker failed to spot the car's revolutionary appeal and missed the urgent competitive questions it should have raised.

Subjective: What's Unsaid?

The final category of questions differs from all the others. Whereas they deal with the substance of a challenge, it deals with the personal reservations, frustrations, tensions, and hidden agendas that can push decision-making off course. Volocopter's CEO, Dirk Hoke, once told us, "When we fail, it's often because we haven't considered the emotional part."

The notion of people issues as a competitive advantage gained prominence in the aviation industry in the early 1980s. Herb Kelleher, then the CEO of Southwest Airlines, recognized that the customer experience could be dramatically improved by putting employees first and empowering them to treat people right. SAS's CEO, Jan Carlzon, transformed the Scandinavian airline by "inverting the pyramid" to support customer-facing staffers in "moments of truth." (See "The Work of Leadership," HBR, December 2001.) In both cases the role of managers became to coach and support—not monitor and control—frontline staff. They learned to ask their *internal* customers, "How can I help?"

If you neglect this mode of questioning or fail to push hard enough in it, your proposed solution might be undone by subjective reactions even though your analysis, insights, and plans are sound. British Airways is a cautionary example. In 1997 it was the world's leading carrier of international passengers, but surveys showed that it was viewed as staid and stuffy. So CEO Robert Ayling and his team decided to boost the airline's global image by replacing the British colors on the planes' tail fins with ethnic designs by artists from around the world.

The designs were visually striking, but the top team badly misgauged employees' and customers' emotional reactions. The staff was distressed that a £60 million rebrand had been undertaken amid ongoing cost-saving measures. British business travelers—the airline's core customers—were strongly attached to the national branding and antagonized by its removal. And as if to underline the error, Virgin CEO Richard Branson announced that his planes would proudly "fly the flag." BA's new designs were withdrawn two years later, and the misjudgment contributed to Ayling's ouster.

Team members may be reluctant to explore emotional issues unless the leader provides encouragement and a safe space for discussion. They may fail to share misgivings simply because no one else is doing so—a social dynamic known as *pluralistic ignorance*. Leaders must invite dissenting views and encourage doubters to share their concerns.

Balancing Your Question Mix

We created a tool to help people assess their questioning styles and gave it to 1,200 global executives. Although the combined results showed an even distribution among the five styles we've

What's Your Question Mix?

The questions below are taken from the self-assessment we use with executives and their teams. Our wording here is very direct to avoid ambiguity, but you'll want to be more diplomatic in practice. Reflect on the five sets of questions and think about which ones come most naturally to you and which feel less comfortable, rating them on a scale of 1 (not part of my repertoire) to 5 (one of my go-tos). Compare the totals for each section and focus your attention on the lowest-scoring sets.

Investigative

What happened?	1	2	3	4	5
What is and isn't working?	1	2	3	4	5
What are the causes of the problem?	1	2	3	4	5
How feasible and desirable is each option?	1	2	3	4	5
What evidence supports our proposed plan?	1	2	3	4	5
TOTAL					

Speculative

What other scenarios might exist?	1	2	3	4	5
Could we do this differently?	1	2	3	4	5
What else might we propose?	1	2	3	4	5
What can we simplify, combine, modify, reverse, or eliminate?	1	2	3	4	5
What potential solutions have we not considered?	1	2	3	4	5
TOTAL					

Productive

What is the next step?	1	2	3	4	5
What do we need to achieve before taking it?	1	2	3	4	5
Do we have the resources to move ahead?	1	2	3	4	5
Do we know enough to proceed?	1	2	3	4	5
Are we ready to decide?	1	2	3	4	5
TOTAL					

Interpretive

What did we learn from this new information?	1	2	3	4	5
What does it mean for our present and future actions?	1	2	3	4	5
What should be our overarching goal?	1	2	3	4	5
How does this fit with that goal?	1	2	3	4	5
What are we trying to achieve?	1	2	3	4	5
TOTAL					

Subjective

How do you really feel about this decision?	1	2	3	4	5
What aspect of it most concerns you?	1	2	3	4	5
Are there differences between what was said, what was heard, and what was meant?	1	2	3	4	5
Have we consulted the right people?	1	2	3	4	5
Are all stakeholders genuinely aligned?	1	2	3	4	5
TOTAL					

described, individual answers revealed major imbalances. One category or another was barely on the radar of more than a third of the executives. And follow-up interviews showed that many leaders were overly attached to the types of questions that had brought them success. They relied on those at the expense of other kinds of inquiries.

Assess your current question style

Self-awareness is an essential first step, of course, toward correcting or compensating for weaknesses. For insight into your questioning preferences and habits, you can take an abridged version of our self-assessment. After you've identified your strong points and weaknesses, three tactics can improve your mix. You can adjust your repertoire of questions, change your emphasis to reflect evolving needs, and surround yourself with people who compensate for your blind spots.

Adjust your repertoire

Having established which types of questions you are most and least comfortable asking, you need to create a better balance. One way to begin is to remind yourself of the five categories before your next decision-making meeting and ensure that you're considering all of them. The CHRO at a large tech company we worked with had us display the framework throughout an important company program.

You can also try out questions from your weak or missing categories in a few low-stakes situations. That will help you understand how things you're not accustomed to asking can open up a discussion. Steven Baert, a former chief people and organization officer at Novartis, described his process on *The Curious Advantage* podcast. "Previously [I focused on] listening to fix," he told the host. "'You have a problem. I need a few points of data from you so I can solve the problem.' [But now] I'm practicing listening to learn."

There's another step involved in adjusting your repertoire: You may need to discard some types of questions that served you well in the past. This point was captured in a *Financial Times* profile of Erick Brimen, CEO of the investment group NeWay Capital, who describes himself as a stubborn, goal-oriented micromanager. "The lesson I've been learning," he said, "is to let go of the 'how to get there' and to focus on 'where we are going.'"

Change your emphasis

Your question mix is a moving target, especially if you're now in a new role, company, or industry. As you take on bigger responsibilities, for instance, you'll face increasingly complex challenges, not just because they have more components but also because you're allowed to take larger leaps. Reflecting on her own trajectory, Patricia Corsi, the chief marketing, digital, and information officer at Bayer Consumer Health, told us, "As your career progresses, you're offered riskier moves, into jobs you've never done, domains you don't know, and challenges you've never experienced. . . . [People] gamble on your ability to ask the questions that will help you learn."

With every job change, you face a challenge to adapt. The question mix that previously worked for you and helped you land your new role might now lead you astray. We spoke with Larry Dominique when he was adjusting to his new position as the SVP and head of Alfa Romeo and Fiat North America. "Drawing on my experience as an engineer, I'll go deeper into costs, resources-management efficiency, and customer satisfaction," he told us. But he recognized the danger of playing only to his established strengths: "I have to remind myself that my real value as a leader is to provide the big picture and to move beyond the questions that are comfortable for me."

Find others who can compensate

As previously noted, you don't need to come up with all the questions yourself; it should be a team effort. José Muñoz, the global president and CEO of Hyundai Motor Company, sometimes delegates the questioner role. "The person who asks the question should be the one who's best equipped," he told us. "As the boss, I might invite someone on my team to continue a line of questioning." After completing his self-assessment, Robert Jasiński, then the managing director of Danone in Romania, said, "I'll pay more attention to what I value the least [the speculative category]. And if someone on my team is a good creative thinker, I'll do a better job of listening to what they have to say."

As a leader, you're responsible for noticing missing perspectives and giving people a chance to contribute. Gilles Morel, the president of Whirlpool Europe, Middle East, and Africa, told us, "I need to make space for the people who aren't like me to ask these questions that I'm not good at asking." But getting everyone to contribute may not be easy. A change of leadership style to a more inquisitive approach can feel threatening. And the same query may elicit either vital input or defensiveness, depending on how it's phrased. One HR specialist finds that "Why?" questions sometimes trigger resistance and that a simple change to "How come . . . ?" gets better results. David Loew, CEO of the biopharmaceutical company Ipsen, told us, "If you start asking closed or loaded questions, such as 'Why have you done it like this?,' it can feel like a police interrogation. That creates an unsafe space, and unease spreads to the rest of the team."

At least as important as the words used are the perceived attitude and intention of the questioner. The question "Is everyone OK with that?," for example, can be heard as either a genuine invitation to share reservations or an attempt to shut down the discussion. "When I ask searching questions, I make it clear that it's OK if you don't have an answer, or if you don't have one right away," Charles Bouaziz, CEO of the medical technology group MTD, told us. "Your tone often matters more than the question. People sometimes assume you're testing them." Problems of interpretation are exacerbated in virtual meetings, where intention is harder to assess; you can't be sure how your question has landed. "Without the full body cues of in-person meetings, leaders have to lean even more strongly into asking the right questions, and listening for misunderstandings or trigger points," Lisa Curtis, the founder and CEO of Kuli Kuli Foods, wrote in *Inc.* magazine.

You'll need to educate your team about the various kinds of questions and the importance of attending to all of them. Some of the most successful executives we know always start conversations with new people by creating a safe space and demonstrating openness and vulnerability. They operate in what Marilee Adams, the author of *Change Your Questions, Change Your Life* and the founder of the Inquiry Institute, calls "learner mode," as opposed to "judger mode." The former is expansive and focuses on assumptions, possibilities, solutions, and meaningful action. The latter is reactive and shortsighted and focuses on discovering who's to blame.

But even when the entire team contributes, there's no guarantee that all five kinds of questions will be covered, especially in high-stress situations. Team members may have a shared blind spot. If that's the case, try assigning one question type to each member—at least until the group's collective repertoire is reasonably well balanced.

To Gilles Morel, the end goal is clear. "I want to create a questioning muscle within the team," he has said. "I need to set the stage so that my curiosity is amplified by the curiosity of others. Their questions should stimulate my questions." His remarks echo Jensen Huang's belief that leadership involves "getting everybody to ask and answer questions."

. . .

By pinpointing the strengths and weaknesses in your interrogatory styles and considering the five types of questions we've outlined, you and your team can make smarter strategic decisions. You'll be more likely to cover all the critical areas that need to be explored—and you'll surface information, insights, and options you might otherwise have missed.

Originally published in May–June 2024. Reprint R2403C

2

The Uniqueness Trap

by Bent Flyvbjerg, Alexander
Budzier, M.D. Christodoulou
and M. Zottoli

U niqueness bias is what psychologists call the tendency individuals have to think they're more unusual than they actually are. In the field of project management, it manifests itself as the belief that projects are one of a kind. This is partly a conscious choice, stemming from the view that when something is presented as unique and new, it's more likely to attract support and funding. But the bias is also deeply entrenched in the project management profession and the literature about it. The U.S.-based Project Management Institute, for example, defines a project as "a temporary endeavor undertaken to create a unique product, service, or result." The U.K.-based Association for Project Management defines a project similarly, as a "unique, transient endeavor." The very first study of projects as a management problem identified their finite duration as a "unique aspect of the project manager's job." And in his classic book *Development Projects Observed,* Albert O. Hirschman concluded that each project he had studied represented "a unique constellation of experiences and consequences."

To find out how distinctive most projects actually are, we analyzed data on more than 1,300 IT projects in 34 companies, which had budgets ranging from $77,000 to $4.5 billion. We then took a deep dive into 219 of them, which were located in North America, Europe, the Middle East, Africa, Asia, and Australasia, to see whether managers believed that their projects were unique and how that perception affected project performance.

What we found was sobering. Our analysis suggested that managers are indeed highly prone to believing that their projects are one of a kind, even though few, if any, actually are. This causes them to think they have nothing to learn from other projects. Most important, it leads them to underestimate risk and overestimate opportunity and thus make poor decisions. Specifically, the more distinctive managers consider a project to be, the more likely it is to exceed its budget, and the more likely the overrun is to be considerable. That led us to the conclusion that improving project performance has less to do with managing the activities involved and more to do with addressing how project managers make decisions.

In this article we'll look first at the relationship between perceived uniqueness and performance outcomes and show how little grounding the perception of uniqueness has in reality. Then we'll offer a theory about why uniqueness bias occurs and conclude with some advice on how managers can fight against it.

The Cost of Uniqueness Bias

To quantify the effect of perceived uniqueness on projects, we asked the managers of each of the 219 projects in our sample to

Idea in Brief

The Trap

Project planners and managers are primed to see their projects as one of a kind, especially those that are complex and new to them personally. In reality, however, few, if any, projects are unique.

Why It's a Problem

When people assume that their projects have no precedent, they don't look for lessons from other projects. As a result they make poor decisions that lead to significant cost and schedule overruns.

How to Avoid It

Before putting a project plan together, ask people in your company if they've seen anything like it before; if they haven't, look externally for similar projects. If you can't find any direct analogues, break the project down into components, which may be comparable across projects. Then use forecasting and risk assessment methods to reduce other biases that may undermine good decisions.

indicate, on a scale of one to 10, how much they agreed with the statement "This project is unique, and therefore it is difficult to compare with other projects." Twenty-seven percent gave their project a score of seven or higher.

Next we tested the association between perceived uniqueness and performance, which we assessed by measuring the benefits delivered and cost and schedule overruns. The results supported our hypothesis that project leaders' view of projects as unique was correlated with underperformance. We found that a one-point increase on the 10-point scale was associated, on average, with a five-percentage-point increase in cost overruns. That meant that in projects receiving the highest rating—a 10—cost overruns were 45 percentage points higher, on average, than overruns in projects receiving the lowest rating (a one).

Worryingly, in 37% of the projects rated a 10, the cost overrun was extreme—exceeding the budget by more than 75%.

It should be noted that the prior conclusions are based on perceived uniqueness. As we discovered, the perceptions didn't necessarily match reality.

Do Unique Projects Actually Exist?

The short answer is no. In fact, whenever we came across a project we thought was unique, it turned out not to be.

Here's an example: In 2004 the top civil servant in charge of decommissioning nuclear power plants in Sweden needed a reliable estimate of how much that effort, which would take decades, would cost, as well as how expensive it would be to safely store nuclear waste, which would last centuries. The Swedish government was going to ask the nuclear industry to pay into a fund to cover the costs, and it needed to know how much to collect.

The Swedish official approached one of us, Bent Flyvbjerg, for advice. Bent didn't think he could help. At the time he didn't have any data on nuclear decommissioning. No other country had carried out such a program. (Decommissioning nuclear plants has become more common since then.) The project truly did seem unique. But the Swedish official had read an article Bent had written about the costs and cost risks for transportation infrastructure projects involving roads, bridges, tunnels, and rail lines. He proposed using Bent's data as a "floor" and assuming that the real cost risks of nuclear decommissioning would be higher. The Swedish government could get the nuclear industry to start making payments based on the floor and then adjust the estimate and the payments as it learned more about decommissioning. Bent realized that he had fallen into the uniqueness trap by assuming that the manager of a project as unprecedented as nuclear decommissioning would have nothing to learn from other projects. He has never forgotten that lesson.

Were the managers in our sample of IT projects similarly mistaken? We looked at the 59 projects with a perceived uniqueness score of seven or higher and compared their functional scope, descriptions, and start dates against those of 6,219 other projects in another, larger database. We found that with all 59 projects, including those rated a nine or a 10, a similar project had, in fact, previously been executed in the same organization or the same industry. In other words, none of the projects could be considered unique. For example, five of the 59 projects were regulatory-compliance projects in banks. We established not only that each of the banks in question had completed similar regulatory efforts before but also that every other bank in its relevant jurisdiction was working to address the same type of regulation at the same time.

On that basis we concluded that many more projects are perceived as unique than actually are and that perceived and actual uniqueness are not correlated. We also found that perceived uniqueness is what matters to project performance, because when managers think there is nothing to learn from other endeavors, the lack of learning will hamper their projects.

How Uniqueness Bias Happens

Our study suggests that the bias is linked to certain project features. Perceived uniqueness was generally correlated with a project's complexity, its political sensitivity, its number of unknown variables, and the extent to which its requirements shifted. But none of those characteristics had a statistically significant effect on their own, which implied that they could not by themselves explain extreme cost overruns. From a statistical perspective, the uniqueness bias was the cause of the overruns, and despite the correlations, it was not rooted in a project's complexity, sensitivity, uncertainty, or requirements.

So where did the bias come from? One strong possibility is that it resulted from the tendency to assume that what's unique to you will be unique to everyone. For instance, California has never built a high-speed rail line before, so in that sense, the recent efforts to construct one between Los Angeles and San Francisco may be considered unique. But there are plenty of precedents outside California: Dozens of similar rail projects have been built around the world, with data and lessons learned that would be highly valuable to California for assessing costs, schedules, contracting relationships, procurement, revenues, and environmental impact.

Our research appears to confirm that people are more likely to believe that a project is unique if they have no personal experience of anything similar. Consider what happened with the chief information officer of one large global logistics company that participated in our study. When we debriefed the company about its results, the CIO spotted a project described by his managers as absolutely unique, scoring a 10 on our scale. When the CIO asked which project it was, he learned that it was the installation of a standard software package for supply chain and warehouse automation in the Czech Republic. That surprised him because the company had installed this package for clients in nearly 1,000 other locations. He phoned the Czech project manager on the spot to find out what was going on. The manager explained that the project was unique because it was the first time that this software would be used in the Czech Republic.

The uniqueness trap feeds into what the Nobel laureate Daniel Kahneman called the "inside view." When managers fall into it, they will fail to gather data and proven insights that could help them and will build budgets and schedules based only on their own beliefs and personal experiences. That can be risky: Plenty of behavioral research shows that when decision-makers do this, they tend to underestimate not only average risk but also the probability of rare, catastrophic outcomes. Another Nobel laureate, Richard Feynman, famously found that this was precisely what happened in the *Challenger* space shuttle disaster: The inside view of flight risk at NASA, especially among its top managers, was so narrow that it caused the agency to wildly underestimate the chances of an explosion, resulting in the tragic loss of the shuttle with all seven astronauts aboard.

Take an Outside View

The cure for uniqueness bias is to always assume that someone, somewhere has undertaken a project like yours, adopting what Kahneman called the "outside view." Before you start putting your project together, therefore, ask other people in your company if they've seen anything like it before, because chances are that, as we just saw with the logistics firm, someone in your organization has done something comparable.

If you can't find any direct analogues, break the project down into modules and subprocesses, which may then prove comparable across projects. One project leader at a major international bank told us that many of its teams had believed that their projects—especially big IT-led change programs—were unique, but after disassembling them into specific tasks and approaches, they found opportunities to leverage experiences from other projects. As he explained, "If you're developing a run book for a go-live migration, you should talk to people who have done migrations before. Or if you're trying to estimate the lead times in establishing your test environment for a new project, ask other projects and teams for their experiences with lead times to get an outside view, and use this to challenge the inside view of your team."

If you can't find analogues inside your organization, look further afield. At a McKinsey conference for IT leaders we attended, a participant whose company had been involved in the invention and rollout of mobile texting suggested that it had truly been a unique project. The leader explained that it had taken only a few weeks to develop the SMS app and that no one on the project or outside it had really understood what the team had invented. Adoption was slow at first. The project seemed minor. No one could have predicted the explosion in usage that would follow, and no other project had set a precedent for it. So mobile texting was unique in that sense, or so the leader argued, and many of us in the room agreed at first.

But then others jumped in and suggested that texting was not unprecedented. A host of communication technologies could be considered its forerunners, including the telegraph, the radio, the telephone, the fax machine, and early versions of today's internet, such as ARPANET. A systematic study of the diffusion of these and other new communication tools would have given the inventors of texting an idea of the uncertainties and the S-curve growth pattern—with a slow start and acceleration later—that they were likely to face. Had anyone thought about that? No, because everyone saw texting as both unique and unimportant and was therefore not motivated to look for similarities.

Once you have found your analogues, be careful about how you process the information you glean from them. Even when taking an outside perspective, project managers making forecasts and decisions can fall prey to other biases that cause them to discount the risks attached. Fortunately, there are forecasting and risk assessment methods that help eliminate or reduce biases. The main ones are discussed next.

Reference-class forecasting

This is a way to predict the future by looking at what has happened in similar situations. In a project management context, it involves comparing possible outcomes of your project in terms of costs, timeliness, and other performance measures with how all the similar projects performed on the same measures. In other words, to assess the probability of a 10% cost overrun in your project, look at how often a 10% overrun has occurred for the whole class of comparable projects. This approach was first applied in 2004 for a mass transit project in Scotland, and today it's used in hundreds, if not thousands, of projects across business and government.

Similarity-based forecasting

A complementary and more focused tool bases predictions about the performance of a system or a project over time on the past performance of a similar system operating under comparable conditions. Similarity-based forecasting helps managers identify unexpected outcomes and variations in actual operating conditions. It can be applied in many contexts, notably in macroeconomics, where economists believe that drawing on data from situations that match your current conditions produces more accurate forecasts than relying on a more general dataset.

Premortems

In these exercises participants presume that a particular outcome will happen and offer an analysis of why it will occur. For example, before starting a project you might assume that it will be completed 10 months later than forecast and then explain why. Premortems entail what behavioral psychologists call "prospective hindsight," a concept that began to appear in management literature in the wake of a groundbreaking 1989 article by Deborah Mitchell, Edward Russo, and Nancy Pennington. They're a highly effective way of surfacing potential problems. The 1989 research suggests that prospective hindsight can improve decision-making and also make people significantly more proactive.

Noise audits

Kahneman, Andrew Rosenfield, Linnea Gandhi, and Tom Blaser described this technique in the 2016 HBR article "Noise: How to Overcome the High, Hidden Cost of Inconsistent Decision Making." The idea is that human decision-makers are swayed not only by biases but also by "noise"—factors unrelated and irrelevant to the decision being made. A noise audit helps them measure the effects of those factors. It involves presenting multiple decision-makers with a set of similar hypothetical situations and asking them to predict outcomes. For instance, you might ask a group of judges to predict the sentences for a set of similar criminal convictions. The objective is to assess how the predicted sentences of each judge vary across cases as well as how they vary across the group of judges as a whole. Typically, the noise level is the standard deviation of predictions across cases and across the predictors. If it's high, then the judges need to revisit how they make sentencing decisions. The tool can be applied to help project managers identify whether they're likely to be swayed by irrelevant factors in making key decisions in, say, purchasing services or hiring.

These methods, and their effectiveness, are well documented in management literature. Anyone interested in eliminating uniqueness bias and other preconceptions that distort decision-making—which is to say, anyone interested in running projects and organizations successfully—should become versed in them.

. . .

It's easy to understand why people think their projects are unique. It stems from what Kahneman called "fast thinking," which is humans' mental default mode. Fast thinking saves project planners and managers the considerable effort of figuring out which class of project a new undertaking belongs to, what the averages and extremes are for that class, how those values translate into risk, and how that risk may be mitigated. But very few, if any, projects are unique, no matter how complex they are. Unless you accept that and invest in identifying similar endeavors and learning from them, your own project will most likely come in late and well over budget and underdeliver on benefits.

Originally published in March–April 2025. Reprint R2502K

3

Why Multibusiness Strategies Fail and How to Make Them Succeed

by Bharat N. Anand and David J. Collis

Multibusiness enterprises remain the dominant form of corporate organization today. While crafting strategies for them can certainly be hard, the way many leaders go about it is flawed: They focus too much on the composition of their portfolio and too little on how the corporation should add value to the businesses in it. A corporation's scope determines its strategic potential, but aligning its structure and management processes with its chosen sources of value creation determines the success of its execution.

In this article we provide an approach to corporate strategy that addresses all the critical elements—the vision of how to add value, the portfolio choices, and the structure and management processes—in an integrated fashion. It's based on decades of research, case writing, teaching, and work with multibusiness companies. We use the term "multibusiness" to describe a broad set of firms that each own a variety of businesses. At some of them the products sold by the businesses are closely related. At others, including traditional conglomerates—companies composed of largely unrelated businesses—they aren't.

In our view corporate strategies that effectively add value fall on a continuum, and leaders need to decide where their firms are on it. Each choice involves trade-offs and requires specific management processes to support it, making it hard to mix and match elements from different locations on the continuum. That idea has far-reaching implications for the practice of corporate strategy.

A Pressing Need

In the era of technological disruption, large companies constantly feel pressured to spin off or divest legacy businesses and enter new ones with innovative business models. Many are undergoing digital transformations, which often demand a highly coordinated approach to driving change and efficiencies across businesses. Meanwhile competition from nimble, focused start-ups is forcing them to renew their search for synergies.

In this environment the practice of corporate strategy has largely been a failure. Indeed, most multibusiness firms have historically destroyed shareholder value. Studies have shown that they're subject to a "diversification discount": Their market capitalization is, on average, about 15% less than the combined value of their separate businesses, according to research by Philip G. Berger and Eli Ofek and many subsequent studies.

But even while many multibusiness firms struggle (witness the radical shrinking and breakup of General Electric), others

Idea in Brief

The Problem

Multibusiness enterprises often struggle with crafting effective strategies because their leaders focus too much on the composition of their portfolios and not enough on enhancing the businesses in them.

The Result

The market capitalization of many diversified enterprises ends up being less than the combined value of their separate businesses.

The Solution

Strategies for adding value fall on a continuum, and leaders need to decide where their enterprises are on it. Each choice involves trade-offs. Successful multibusiness firms understand this and align their structure and management processes with their sources of value creation across the portfolio.

are thriving. They include companies operating in traditional businesses (like Danaher Corporation), top-tier private equity firms (like Blackstone and KKR), and tech giants (like Amazon and Tencent). One might say their success is just luck. It's not. Even though multibusiness firms underperform *on average*, a large fraction—nearly 40%—consistently outperform their peers or the market, according to a 2014 study of more than 8,000 firms Bharat did with Dmitri Byzalov. Poor performance by multibusiness firms isn't a law of nature.

Why are some firms able to overcome the liability of diversification while others are not? How are they able to succeed? What sets them apart in the choices they make and in how they manage their businesses? By exploring these questions, we have gleaned lessons that other corporations can apply to improve their execution of strategy.

The Logic of the Possible

Let's start with a reminder of how multibusiness firms create value. Consider this simple example:

A firm has four lines of business, each with a different return on investment (r). The relative size—or weight (w)—of each business in the portfolio differs too. Together, the returns and weights determine overall corporate performance (P):

$$P = w1 \times r1 + w2 \times r2 + w3 \times r3 + w4 \times r4 - \text{corporate overhead}$$

How can the corporation increase overall value? Logically, there are only four ways: First, improve the performance of each business (the r's) in isolation. Let's call this a "vertical" approach to adding value, since it primarily involves interactions that headquarters has with the individual businesses—including strategic guidance, the selection of top management, and the choice of performance incentive schemes. Second, increase the synergies between the business units. We call this a "horizontal" strategy, since it involves connections across the businesses—the transferring of skills and resources like talent, brand power, and best practices, or the sharing of operational activities like centralized production and distribution networks. Third, change the weights of each business in the portfolio. That will involve buying and selling businesses or reallocating resources among them. And fourth, minimize corporate overhead.

Cut through the rhetorical clutter—the corporate references to strategies as M&A-led, organic growth, disruptive innovation, customer-centric, and so on—and all approaches boil down to one of the four described. These are the only ways to add value.

A lot of corporations pay disproportionate attention to the assembly of the portfolio of businesses (changing the w's). This happens for two reasons: Self-interested bankers and consultants promote it, and it's concrete and observable and has an immediate impact. All too often executives give short shrift to the ongoing management of the portfolio (changing the r's), but ultimately it's how the value of any set of businesses is realized and improved over the long term.

Now, you may ask, can a company be effective in pursuing all these approaches simultaneously? If not, why not? And are particular strategies better than others? Let's examine those questions next.

The Strategy Continuum

As you move across our strategy continuum, the businesses in a corporation's portfolio become increasingly related. (See the exhibit "The strategy continuum.") At one extreme is a company whose portfolio can include any kind of business, regardless of the products or services it delivers; at the other extreme is a company whose businesses have many similarities, such as related products, common distribution channels, and shared technologies.

Clorox is an example of a company that falls on the highly related, or far right, end of the spectrum. It sells a limited range of branded grocery-store items, from bleach to Hidden Valley Ranch dressing to Kingsford charcoal. Its major competitors are private labels, so the strategic challenge with all its offerings is how to drive consumer demand with superior product performance. Clorox's businesses traditionally use brick-and-mortar retail channels, and they share a supply chain that can drive efficiencies and a brand management group that supports each product. Senior managers typically "grow up" in the businesses

The strategy continuum

A diversified company's place along the continuum is determined by how related the businesses in its portfolio are. Each position along the spectrum has a separate logic for value creation and calls for different choices about organizational structure, methods of monitoring and controlling the businesses, the size of the corporate center, and the activities through which it adds value.

Methods of adding value: PRIMARY / SECONDARY / NONE

LEAST RELATED → MOST RELATED

	Government Pension Fund Global	Berkshire Partners	Danaher	Disney	Clorox
Shared activities					
Supply chain					Primary
Channels					Primary
R&D					Primary
Customers				Secondary	Secondary
Brand				Primary	Secondary
Common processes and skills					
Talent development			Primary	Primary	Primary
Culture			Primary	Primary	Primary
Management toolbox			Primary	Primary	Secondary
Strategy setting			Primary	Primary	Secondary
Policies for incentives, governance, and control					
Capital reallocation		Primary	Primary		
Rigorous performance reviews		Primary	Primary		
High-powered incentives		Primary	Primary		
Portfolio selection					
Buying and selling companies	Primary	Primary			

Strategic choices for:

Organizational structure	DIVISION →	FUNCTIONAL/MATRIX
Control methods	FINANCIAL →	OPERATING
Headquarters size	SMALL →	LARGE

and remain very close to operations—even in the weeds—monitoring supermarket channel sales of brands on a nearly daily basis. The result is a corporate strategy that delivers value across a set of product businesses that have common operational characteristics and can be jointly optimized for success.

Disney is a little farther left on the spectrum. For many decades it has created value for an array of family entertainment businesses by leveraging its franchise characters, such as Mickey Mouse and Buzz Lightyear, across a variety of distribution platforms. The constant development of memorable branded content provides a competitive advantage for every one of its businesses. How much extra would you pay for a Simba toy lion over a similar plush toy (probably one made in the same Chinese factory)? How much of a premium would you pay to stay at one of the Disney hotels in Florida, just so you could have breakfast with Belle, Mulan, and Princess Jasmine? While the businesses differ enough operationally that they need to be structured separately, the parent must still have strong oversight of content quality, coordinate the use of characters across the businesses, and maintain control of the shared brand.

In the middle of the spectrum is Danaher, a classic conglomerate. Over time its businesses have ranged from hand tools to medical devices, environmental equipment, diagnostics, and life sciences. While there are few product or operational synergies among them, all Danaher businesses use the same processes for strategy formulation, breakthrough goal setting, aligning strategic plans with annual and daily operations, and performance reviews. They also leverage a vast set of common tools for incorporating the customer's voice, product planning, identifying growth opportunities, and more. Collectively these tools and processes are called the Danaher Business System

(DBS), and they drive continuous improvement in every business. The corporate center makes M&A decisions, allocates resources across the businesses, serves as an internal consultant, and most important, evangelizes DBS in a disciplined and unrelenting manner.

Berkshire Partners, a private equity firm, is on the unrelated side of the spectrum. Its businesses have been even more diverse than Danaher's; they've included fitness platforms, ethnic foods, mobile phone insurance, car wash systems, and wireless towers. Like other PE firms, Berkshire sees no synergies or connections across its businesses. Indeed, each company in a PE firm's portfolio is legally separate, with limited liability, and other than sharing a parent may have nothing in common with the other ventures in the portfolio. So how do PE firms add value? Typically, through stronger governance, higher-powered incentives (debt and equity), arguably longer horizons, and tighter financial monitoring (including independent boards for each business) than companies are normally used to. While such "vertical" interventions alone don't offer meaningful value-creation possibilities to all businesses, they do to many. As a result the PE model has grown in importance in the economy for more than 30 years. In fact, today PEs oversee businesses accounting for about 6.5% of total U.S. GDP.

The highly unrelated, or far left, end of the spectrum is anchored by corporations that change only the w's and not the r's of companies in their portfolio. They achieve this simply by buying and selling shares in companies. Examples include investment funds and sovereign wealth funds. Unlike private equity firms, these companies generally don't intervene in operating decisions made by the firms they buy and sell. They don't try to achieve any linkages across the businesses in their portfolios;

their success in generating superior returns depends only on a unique ability to identify and make good investments. This requires a strategy for hiring talent, organizing investment teams, and rewarding portfolio managers—none of which affect portfolio companies' actions or interdependencies. And all of this can be achieved at minimal expense.

Take the Norwegian sovereign wealth fund, the Government Pension Fund Global. Under a CEO and an executive team, it invests $1.6 trillion across equities, real estate, renewable energy structure, and bonds, with different product managers responsible for each category of asset. The entire corporation employs fewer than 600 people, or roughly one employee per $3 billion in assets under management.

Each of these enterprises represents a different logic for value creation along the continuum. As a result, they embody very different choices about organizational structure, methods of monitoring and controlling the businesses, what the corporate center does, and the role and size of the parent. Yet despite these strikingly different approaches to managing multiple businesses, all five companies (and others like them) have performed impressively over extended periods of time.

The Art of the Possible: Lessons for Managing Multibusiness Companies

Multibusiness enterprises must make choices in three core areas: the underlying corporate resources and capabilities that add value to the portfolio, the businesses that belong in the portfolio, and, most critical, organizational design and management processes.

The decisions made in each area affect the decisions made in the others. How a corporation is organized, for example, will enhance or limit its ability to add value to a business. A divisional structure, in which businesses are independent, will increase product focus, managerial autonomy, and entrepreneurialism but limit cross-product synergies. Functional structures and matrix structures (in which functions span multiple businesses and report to both business-unit and functional executives) prioritize efficiency and synergy over the accountability of the individual businesses. None of these choices are better than the others—they simply are different.

This leads us to the most important lesson: There is no one best corporate strategy. Indeed, any strategy along the continuum can be successful provided that the corporation adopts the organizational practices appropriate to its position on it. And each model has risks and limits. Even if the value that can be added by sharing more activities is potentially greater on the highly related end of the continuum, so too are the costs incurred from intervening in the operations of businesses. Success comes from knowing where the firm is on the continuum and aligning its choices accordingly.

As a corollary, best practices for how to add value do not exist either. Debates about the merits of, say, related versus unrelated diversification, collaborative versus competitive cultures, or flexible alliance-type structures versus fully owned ones are ultimately misleading, since the right choices about these things almost always depend on the firm's location on the continuum.

Some Common Mistakes

Though the logic for multibusiness strategy seems straightforward, in practice companies appear to systematically fall into a few traps.

Overestimating synergies

For a variety of reasons, companies often focus too much on capturing synergies. Sometimes they want to justify their chosen scope; sometimes it seems easier to exploit observable, tangible sources of synergy (through shared activities) than to pursue less tangible benefits; and sometimes their leaders mistakenly believe that more integration is always better and underestimate the costs of achieving it. At many companies tables cataloging the extent of synergies across businesses or functions, with dark circles representing high synergy and blank circles indicating none, reinforce this misconception by suggesting that blank circles need to be filled in. Instead, companies would do better to recognize that certain synergies may be best left unexploited because chasing them can increase coordination costs and discourage entrepreneurialism, ultimately compromising the strategic model.

Management's tasks increase as you move from the far left (highly unrelated) to the far right (highly related) along the continuum, and the design of organizations needs to reflect that. If product divisions share very little, there need not be any organizational overlap. When divisions have many activities in common, the need to integrate shared functions can outweigh the advantages of specialization. However, the loss of autonomy can make units less entrepreneurial and less accountable. This is the classic trade-off between centralization and decentralization.

This trade-off explains why Newell Brands kept manufacturing, R&D, and branding separate across its product businesses for a long time despite large opportunities for synergistic integration. Similarly, Danaher only recently introduced a shared purchasing function. At the highly related end of spectrum, in contrast, we've seen a huge chemical company create a matrix structure that left only 40% of the costs of a business under each unit's direct control.

Rather than going through synergies category by category—back office, culture, process, employees, costs, channel, brand, customer strategy—and trying to maximize them all, figure out the model (the position on the continuum) that's right for you and then understand where you should and should not capture synergies. Sometimes forgoing them can be the best path to creating more long-term value. Maximizing alignment can be better than maximizing synergies.

The portfolio fixation

As we've noted, companies often focus too much on the business composition of the portfolio. As one of the few initiatives that can help leaders move the dial in a substantive way, portfolio reconfiguration—making an acquisition, spinning off a business, pursuing a new, disruptive model—has been a favorite tool of CEOs. Advice from investment bankers, activist shareholders, consulting firms, lawyers, and private equity firms tends to heighten their inclination to use it. These players will articulate a good reason for expanding the portfolio, only to then advance equally good reasons to shrink it. Analyst reports, for instance, can be dangerously misleading, implying that portfolio gaps vis-à-vis competitors ought to be filled. (See the exhibit "Beware of comparisons of companies' businesses.") The choice of portfolio is, as we've seen, only one of the ingredients of a successful multibusiness strategy.

The evolution of the AT&T–Time Warner merger is illustrative. The synergy argument for the deal, which was announced in 2016 and completed in 2018, included the possibility of new content offerings on mobile devices, better targeting of advertising

Beware of comparisons of companies' businesses

Analyst reports containing tables like this one—comparing media and entertainment companies—imply that portfolio gaps vis-à-vis competitors ought to be filled. That idea can be dangerous because it's not simply the number of businesses in the portfolio that determines a diversified company's success. The logic of value creation, organizational structure, and management processes matters, too.

Businesses	Media and entertainment companies							
	A	B	C	D	E	F	G	H
Linear TV	■	■	■	■		■	■	■
Movies	■	■	■	■		■	■	
Streaming	■	■	■	■	■	■	■	■
Cable channel	■		■		■	■		
Music	■		■		■			
Publishing	■		■					■
Theme parks	■	■	■					
Cable network		■	■					
Hardware					■			
Internet		■						

using information on content views, and new content-and-wireless-subscription bundles. Each of those things required deeper connections between advertising, content, and communications. Yet the postmerger organizational structure set up separate units for each, making it hard to exploit those synergies. Adding to the troubles, the media and technology businesses had markedly different cultures. AT&T sold Time Warner less than four years after the merger, underscoring our point: How you manage the portfolio of businesses is as important as its initial selection.

Benchmarking gone awry

Emulating the choices of competitors is one of the longest-standing management practices. But the failure to recognize that those choices are invariably contextual—even companies in the same industry might be pursuing different corporate strategies—can lead companies astray. For example, copying a competitor's move to downsize corporate headquarters in an effort to become leaner is a common trap. There's a reason that there's such a range of headquarters sizes. There is no one right size, since the roles that headquarters has to perform vary from company to company. A successful financial services company with 10,000 employees and a large IT function might have 1,000 people at headquarters, whereas a successful private equity firm might employ 10 professionals there. The corporate center will necessarily be much larger in companies at the highly related end of the spectrum, where its horizontal coordinating tasks become much more demanding.

How to Design a Multibusiness Strategy

Asking the following questions can help you and your team create a successful multibusiness strategy.

What is the corporate vision?

How can the parent company add value across the business portfolio? How can we improve the competitive advantage of our business units in their markets, and what is the logic behind those moves—the theory for why the whole can exceed the sum of the parts?

More specific questions will help you flesh the vision out: Where on the product-relatedness continuum do we lie as a company or intend to? What assets will be shared across the businesses, and which should not be shared? What is the unique glue that connects the businesses in the portfolio and improves the competitive advantage of each (the way Mickey Mouse and other animated cartoon characters do for Disney's theme parks, hotels, toys, and cable channel)? Sometimes the answer to this last question can seem rather generic but isn't (the stock-picking ability of Warren Buffett); other times it can appear complex but isn't unique (economies from combining manufacturing operations, which others can exploit equally well).

Broad portfolios can sometimes have a surprisingly straightforward logic for a more valuable whole. Consider Tencent, China's leading internet company, which operates in a staggeringly large number of businesses, including instant messaging, social networks, multiplayer games, e-commerce, and digital media. On the face of it, they may seem rather different. Yet the glue that binds them all is simple: leveraging deep connections between customers, both within and across each business. Tencent does this effectively and relentlessly.

The corporate vision involves more than choosing a model: It requires matching the potential set of synergies with the actual resources available and assessing the costs of achieving them. In many cases you will have to build the resources you need. After all, a primary task of the CEO is to ensure investment in the unique competences and resources the portfolio will be assembled around. Bob Iger, for example, recommitted to producing high-quality, branded entertainment content as the key to creating value across Disney's businesses, an approach that had always underpinned its success.

Defining the corporate vision typically requires both discipline and creativity. Many companies struggle with this task or sidestep it altogether. This happens for a few reasons: In addition to looking to maximize synergies but failing to recognize the trade-offs from doing so, companies often undervalue process synergies, which can be as potent as product synergies. Or they tie themselves up in simplistic debates about whether the company should be more centralized or more decentralized, instead of parsing which activities or functions merit centralization or coordination and which don't. Decentralized organizations in particular can struggle because they invariably think that an overarching vision is somehow inconsistent with giving units independence.

What is the right portfolio and organizational structure?

Once the corporate vision has been articulated, it has immediate implications for the set of businesses that lend themselves to it and how the company should be organized to realize synergies.

The organizational design should strike a balance between business unit autonomy and coordination that fits the company's position on the continuum. At the unrelated end, a structure made up of independent units run by entrepreneurial managers with a minimum of corporate intervention, for instance, allows specialization and maximizes the stand-alone performance of businesses. At the other end, where shared activities become an important source of value creation, the structure is typically functional or a matrix of functional and operating units, enabling greater coordination.

Hand in hand with structures go incentives: how to appropriately monitor and reward each unit (whether it's a business, a geography, or a function). To hold managers accountable and motivate them to improve results, every corporation needs a performance management system. But there is a profound difference between the appropriate metrics for managers at the two ends of the continuum. When the portfolio includes a range of unrelated businesses, a small headquarters staff cannot have the insight or experience to evaluate much more than performance on financial targets. In contrast, when corporate management has a lot of experience in similar businesses, it can evaluate the actions taken by unit managers with operating metrics. At Clorox, for example, corporate management can study daily reports of sales through distribution channels.

In practice, it may take a lot of iterating to align the vision, the portfolio, and the structure. And when making choices about all three, executives need to respect a company's existing culture and heritage. Increasing synergy, after all, requires a structure that enables greater coordination but can also imply less business freedom; recognizing that and calibrating it against the company's culture is important.

What are the right processes?

Even more central to corporate success are the managerial processes that characterize different positions along the continuum. These underpin the day-to-day management of the company and help define its culture.

Every parent's headquarters must fulfill certain basic functions: strategy setting, financial reporting, audit and tax, external relations, capital raising, and oversight by corporate executives. But these can be done, surprisingly, with a very small office. Look at PE firms. Silver Lake, for example, employs 500,000 in its portfolio companies and has fewer than 200 professionals in its headquarters.

Moving toward the relatedness side of the spectrum, the role of headquarters starts to encompass M&A decisions and spinoffs.

It also includes resource allocation: whether and how, for example, more resources should be moved into higher-profit industries. Danaher shifted its resources away from its original tool and transportation industries and into high-tech and medical-technology sectors, one of the keys to its long-term success.

Further along on the continuum, horizontal process sharing becomes important in adding value to the units. It might include transferring resources like brands as well as know-how and management practices. The disciplined application of good management practices can add a remarkable amount of value to otherwise independent business units where few activities are shared and operational synergies are small. Corporate HR can play a crucial role here. Developing a cadre of executives with relevant expertise and moving them across businesses or functions will ensure that unique corporate capabilities are leveraged throughout the organization. Even with this model, though, a small corporate unit can be effective. Rather than following the bad old days in which the corporate staff wrote 500-page manuals whose rules were enforced and audited throughout the organization, companies are now creating "centers of excellence" that serve as internal consultants assisting each business in adopting state-of-the-art practices.

Activity sharing is often perceived as the most obvious source of synergy across businesses. But even there, it must be aligned with the correct structure and control system to be effective. Units that share a manufacturing site, for example, will lose control of their production operations, but that is the price they have to pay for benefiting from scale economies. As the value of sharing activities increases, so do costs of coordination and the size of the headquarters function, making activity sharing appropriate only at the highly related end of the continuum.

What are the right reporting relationships and managerial mindsets?

These can vary considerably across the continuum too. On one extreme the parent acts as a *police officer* with full authority to mandate and control activity in every business unit, ranging from cash management to safety, health, and environmental compliance. Alternatively, it can be a *partner*—serving as a coach or a consultant to the business units, perhaps with a corporate center of excellence that develops but does not compel the adoption of best practices. Or it can be an internal *provider* of shared services, treating the business units as customers and negotiating agreements with them and even allowing them to go outside the corporation for services if desired.

It's critical for corporate staff members to understand which of the three roles they play in interactions with business unit executives. Leadership roles and attitudes in business units can be quite different from those at the parent organization, making transitions challenging for executives moving into jobs at headquarters. And any single corporate function can fall into all three categories or roles. The HR department, for example, may be a police officer when organizing succession plans for the top 100 executives in the company, a partner when setting the structure of compensation in every business unit, and a service provider when administering a corporatewide 401(k) platform.

What should the size of headquarters be?

The answers to the previous four questions will dictate the answer to this question. But leadership should avoid focusing too much on it because the size of the corporate center, by itself, reveals little. It should also never be set by copying companies with a very different corporate strategy.

. . .

The sequencing of these five questions is key to getting multi-business strategy right. Start by having clarity on the company's corporate vision and model—and where it lies on the relatedness continuum. Hoping that a corporate vision or strategy emerges from the ground up never works.

It's also important to recognize that companies can—and do—move along the continuum over time. As the external environment changes—shifting technologies create new business models and opportunities, and competitors improve capabilities—the strategic vision and logic can change, and as a result the organizational design and management of the company must change as well.

A.P. Moller–Maersk, the Danish shipping and logistics company, for example, has made two moves along the continuum in the past 15 years. Under Nils Andersen, its CEO from 2007 to 2016, the company shifted from a tightly integrated and centralized firm to a structure of independent divisions, establishing arm's-length agreements between the shipping line and the container terminal business and substantially reducing the role and size of corporate headquarters. Later, after divesting its oil and gas businesses and refocusing on shipping and logistics, Andersen's successor, Søren Skou (who served as CEO through 2022), reintegrated the business units (a move to the right), and the corporate staff's roles increased. Recently the headquarters in Copenhagen has been expanded to accommodate a larger number of executives. Interestingly, both moves were successful. Despite the difficulty in execution, both CEOs understood the need to align the corporation's structure, systems, and processes with the overall corporate strategy.

The evolution of General Electric and its recent breakup represent a move to the left. For decades, GE was heralded as the paragon of a successful diversified company. But the synergies it enjoyed when it was an industrial giant disappeared as it expanded into entertainment, capital markets, and health care. Despite this, it maintained a management structure, including a large headquarters staff, designed to exploit sources of value that no longer existed.

After becoming GE's CEO, in 2018, Larry Culp, the former head of Danaher, put "focus before synergy." He divested several businesses and turned the three remaining ones—energy generation, aerospace, and health care—into separate publicly traded companies, each now free to adopt the management processes suitable for its own multibusiness strategies. GE Aerospace, which Culp continues to lead, has a headquarters staff of fewer than 200 people.

The lesson in all that is this: The hard part of multibusiness strategy isn't identifying synergies or selecting the portfolio. It's management. Too often, multibusiness companies fail because they get this wrong. They devote their energies to trying to maximize synergies wherever possible instead of recognizing that forgoing some of them can make their jobs easier. They concentrate on tangible, observable things like headquarters size and organizational structure rather than on the day-to-day processes and mindsets that determine success. But when they get it right—understanding where they are on the strategy continuum, aligning their management processes with their structure and sources of value—everything works. The result is outsize shareholder value creation, clarity of purpose, and effective execution.

Originally published in September–October 2024. Reprint R2405K

One Company A/B Tested Hybrid Work. Here's What It Found.

by Nicholas Bloom, James Liang, and Ruobing Han

Amazon's recent call for employees to return to the office (RTO) five days a week is just one example of high-profile companies pulling back from their remote-work policies. RTO advocates often cite the importance of in-person connections, with former Google CEO Eric Schmidt even claiming in a talk at Stanford University, "Google decided that work-life balance and going home early and working from home was more important than winning."

Our real-world study, which randomly assigned employees to a three-day or five-day in-office schedule, provided hard evidence on the benefits of hybrid work when it comes to reducing turnover and increasing profits. Indeed, the results were so strong that the company's middle managers reversed their previously skeptical views on working from home.

Experiment Results

The company we worked with was Trip.com, one of the world's largest online travel companies, with 40,000 employees. One of us, James, is a cofounder and chairman of the company.

Approximately 1,600 China-based employees in marketing, finance, accounting, and engineering volunteered for the study and were randomized into two groups based on whether their birthdays fell on even or odd dates. One group, the control group, went into the office five days a week for six months. The other group, the treatment group, went to the office only on Mondays, Tuesdays, and Thursdays within the same time frame. The company designed the hybrid work schedule in this way to encourage collaboration.

We analyzed data from the six-month experiment and subsequent performance reviews for the next two years and found the two groups showed no differences in productivity, performance-review grade, or promotion.

Before the experiment, managers estimated that hybrid would reduce productivity by 2.6%. After the six-month experiment, they estimated it increased productivity by 1%. Those working under the hybrid model had a higher satisfaction rate and 35% lower attrition. Quit-rate reductions were largest for female employees. Nonmanagers and those with commutes longer than 1.5 hours also had significantly reduced quit rates under hybrid.

According to the Society for Human Resource Management, each quit costs companies at least 50% of an employee's annual salary, which for Trip.com would mean $30,000 for each quit. In Trip.com's experiment, employees liked hybrid so much that their quit rates fell by more than a third—and saved the company millions of dollars a year.

Idea in Brief

The Problem

Since the pandemic, executives have had an ongoing debate about remote work. Many companies are reconsidering their work-from-home policies, but they have no real data on whether hybrid work reduces turnover or increases profits.

The Solution

A six-month experiment conducted by Trip.com showed that employees who worked from home three days a week experienced higher satisfaction and lower attrition rates compared with their colleagues who worked from the office. This reduction in turnover saved millions of dollars in recruiting and training costs, thereby increasing profits for the company.

The Benefits

Business leaders can learn valuable lessons from this study to implement a successful hybrid work model: establishing rigorous performance management systems, coordinating team- or company-level hybrid schedules, and securing support from firm leadership. Additionally, executives should A/B test their own management practices to find what works best for them.

Managerial Lessons

After our study came out in *Nature*, executives were very interested in finding out more. We think there are three critical ingredients that contributed to the success of hybrid working at Trip.com.

First, Trip.com has a rigorous performance management system that's on par with best practices around the world. Managers don't hover over employees at their desks to check their progress or give ad hoc feedback once a year. Instead, the company has an extensive performance-review process every six months to help employees correct course in real time. Employee performance data, as well as feedback from coworkers, clients, direct reports, and managers, are synthesized into a detailed, multidimension performance review on a five-point scale. Through a bell curve appraisal system that ensures a range of grades, Trip.com can effectively recognize and reward the top performers while identifying the bottom ones, who are then placed on performance improvement plans. Moreover, pay and promotions are directly linked to the review. So, the company's managers can effectively motivate and reward high-performing employees whether they work from home or in the office.

Second, in Trip.com's approach to hybrid work, employees have a clear, coordinated schedule of when their team will be in the office together. This prevents the frustration of coming into an empty office only to participate in Zoom calls they could have easily done from home. Trip.com enables all employees to work from home on Wednesdays and Fridays. Other businesses might choose to set their in-office days at the team or company level, but clear schedules are critical for successful hybrid policies.

Finally, Trip.com's CEO and the full executive suite support a hybrid policy. As is common in many modern management practices, from lean manufacturing to organizational agility, having leadership buy-in is critical to support a successful strategy.

"At Trip.com Group, we are dedicated to unlocking the full potential of our employees," said Jane Sun, CEO of Trip.com Group, the parent company listed on NASDAQ. "Our hybrid work model, refined over a decade of innovation and experimentation, is designed to support both personal and professional excellence. We remain committed to fostering an environment where everyone can thrive."

The Value of A/B Testing

One other lesson that managers can take from our study is the value of organizational A/B testing. We've all been subject to

A/B experiments probably dozens of times when using online services, but doing A/B tests with management practices is far rarer.

Trip.com has a tradition of A/B experimentation on management practices going back more than a decade, using these to continuously improve its productivity. For example, back in 2010 it ran experiments on remote working for call-center employees. The current study involved a more diverse group—computer engineers, accounting, marketing, and finance. And with positive results, the leadership took hybrid to the whole company.

Trip.com has been highly data-driven in its decision-making to avoid jumping to incorrect conclusions about the productivity of the hybrid work model. The data showed hybrid employees were working about 1.5 hours less per home-day, superficially suggesting these employees were working less. But a closer examination of the data indicated that hybrid employees put in longer hours on their office days and weekends to make up. Employees shared that they found home-days useful for important activities like a doctor's appointment, taking their children to school or on trips, or leisure activities like golf. Because these workers were well motivated by rigorous performance evaluations, they made up for this with longer hours on office days and weekends.

Trip.com is also conducting more experiments to collect data in other hybrid-related aspects, such as fine-tuning the number of days in the office to find the optimal balance. The benefits of happier workers and better retention make it all very attractive.

Our results showed that under a hybrid work policy, Trip.com was able to generate millions of dollars of profits by reducing expensive attrition without any impact on performance, innovation, or productivity. Firms should expand their A/B testing from consumer experience to daily practices for continuous managerial improvement. Only companies that continually innovate and improve will survive—and to do that, they need to experiment and refine their own management practices.

Adapted from hbr.org, October 29, 2024. Reprint H08DMP

4

Build a Corporate Culture That Works

by Erin Meyer

t the beginning of my career, I worked for the health-care-software specialist HBOC. One day, a woman from human resources came into the cafeteria with a roll of tape and began sticking posters on the walls. They proclaimed in royal blue the company's values: "Transparency, Respect, Integrity, Honesty." The next day we received wallet-sized plastic cards with the same words and were asked to memorize them so that we could incorporate them into our actions. The following year, when management was indicted on 17 counts of conspiracy and fraud, we learned what the company's values really were.

Ever since Peter Drucker famously declared that "culture eats strategy for breakfast," there has been a widespread understanding that managing corporate culture is key to business success.

Editor's Note: This article cites a quotation attributed to Peter Drucker, "culture eats strategy for breakfast." Although this saying is frequently attributed to Drucker, the accuracy of the attribution has been disputed.

Yet few companies articulate their corporate culture in such a way that the words become an organizational reality that guides employee behavior. Which raises the question: If culture eats strategy for breakfast, how should you be cooking it?

I have been studying culture in organizations in my roles as a professor and as an adviser to businesses for the past 20 years. I have looked at companies that have struggled to build cultures that shape the behavior of their employees—and at a few that seem to have cracked the code. In this article I draw on that experience to offer six simple guidelines to help managers who are confronting the challenges of culture building.

1. Build Your Culture Based on Real-World Dilemmas

One of the biggest mistakes companies make when articulating their desired organizational culture is to focus on abstract absolute positives (integrity, respect, trust, and so on). Take integrity. Virtually all leaders want their employees to behave with it. Indeed, there is really no credible alternative to integrity as an articulated value. Never have I come across an organization that said, "In this company, we are all about corruption."

When you articulate your culture using absolute positives, it makes a statement, but it's unlikely to drive the day-to-day decision-making (and therefore the behavior) of your workforce. The trick to making a desired culture come alive is to debate and articulate it using dilemmas. If you identify the tough dilemmas your employees routinely face and clearly state how they should be resolved—"In this company, when we come across this dilemma, we turn left"—then your desired culture will take root and influence the behavior of the team.

Here is one example that I have used in my own work.

Idea in Brief

The Problem

There's a widespread understanding that managing corporate culture is key to business success. Yet few companies articulate their corporate culture in such a way that the words become an organizational reality that molds employee behavior as intended.

What Usually Happens

All too often a culture is described as a set of anodyne norms, principles, or values, which do not offer decision-makers guidance on how to make difficult choices when faced with conflicting but equally defensible courses of action.

How to Fix It

Follow six rules: Ground your culture in the dilemmas you are likely to confront, dilemma-test your values, communicate your values in colorful terms, hire people who fit, let culture drive strategy, and know when to pull back from a value.

Dilemma:

You manage a small team of eight marketing specialists. The team is hardworking and collaborative. Yet you have been in discussions with your boss about a possible organizational change that might take place in four months, which would have a significant impact on your department. Employees would be shuffled around with new bosses and teammates. Some might be asked to move to new locations. This is about 60% likely to happen. Will you share this information with your team now?

Option A: Lean toward team stability. Keep quiet for now. Your team is in a groove. You don't know if the changes will happen. If you tell your employees, they are likely to panic and become distracted, leading to stress and wasted time. Some team members might decide to leave the group in search of stability. Why cause worry and distraction when so much is unknown?

Option B: Lean toward transparency. Tell them what you know. When you are up-front with your employees, it breeds trust. If you were in their shoes, you would want to know. You seek to treat employees like adults, leading them to behave like adults. Adults can handle (and deserve) the truth. Why wait and allow rumors or whispered half-truths to circulate?

Both options are credible and defensible responses to the dilemma. I've presented it to hundreds of managers in dozens of organizations, and I've found that about 45% choose to share the information, and just over half lean toward keeping the information quiet for now.

In which direction would you like your managers to lean? If your goal is stability, you want managers to choose the first option. Tell them, "In this company, our goal is to keep all employees sheltered from distraction. We have a lot to get done, and everyone should be laser-focused on the task at hand." If your organization wants to foster a culture that's all about transparency, tell your workforce, "In this company, our leaders share information like crazy. Even when the cost is inefficiency or distraught feelings, we tell you what we know."

When employees face situations with various credible responses, they can either make a choice based on personal preference or be guided by the culture of the company. When developing your culture, consider those moments when your employees face critical decision-making dilemmas, vigorously debate potential responses, and create value statements that will clearly guide employees' actions.

2. Move Your Culture from Abstraction to Action

If you are building your culture from scratch, debate it using dilemmas from the beginning. But if you already have a stated culture consisting of abstract principles in place, "dilemma-test" them to determine whether they are actionable enough to be useful in real decision-making situations.

I recently advised an online marketplace for tutors and students while it was developing its company culture. I'll call it TutorX. We began by looking at how other companies described their organizational cultures on their websites. The majority defined their culture by listing abstract principles. We put some of them through a "stress test," imagining real-life dilemmas that they could help solve. For example, an international health-care conglomerate stated two of its values—care and meaning—on its website:

> *It's simple. We care. How we work is just as important as the work we do. We help and respect each other.*
>
> *What you do matters. We set out every day to do purposeful work. Our mission is a reminder of why we foster a culture where you can grow, make an impact, and are empowered to bring new ideas.*

The words were not overly broad clichés (such as integrity or respect). The description resonated. Yet we had trouble imagining the on-the-ground dilemmas they could help resolve. Well-intentioned employees asking themselves whether to do meaningless or meaningful work didn't make sense. And surely very few managers were struggling with the question, "Should I show my team that I care or that I don't care?" The principles were clear, but they didn't address real-world choices that employees would routinely face.

Other companies aced the dilemma test. Consider Amazon's value statement: "Have a backbone: Disagree and commit." The second part was coined by a cofounder of Sun Microsystems, Scott McNealy, in the 1980s, and together the six words help Amazon employees resolve actual dilemmas. For example: Your boss is considering three designs for a new ad campaign. You hate the design that she is leaning toward. Should you tell her and make your case against it? Option A: Yes! State your position as clearly and persuasively as possible. Option B: No! You don't want to risk irritating your supervisor or ruining your relationship with her. Which should you choose? The value "Have a backbone" clearly guides your response: Speak up and make your case.

Another example is Pixar's value "Regularly share unfinished work." It's easy to imagine a scenario employees would face.

Dilemma:

You are a film cartoonist in the storm of creation. Some of what you've done is good, but not all of it is fleshed out. Should you keep working until you reach perfection before you share?

Option A: Yes! Why waste others' time and show flaws when you haven't completed what you can do yourself?

Option B: No! You need feedback early to consider multiple perspectives and avoid going down a path that you might later find wasn't the best.

Pixar's stated value resolves the dilemma. Share your work now!

When TutorX put its own culture statements through the dilemma test, there were some for which no one could identify actual dilemmas they would resolve. Those were discarded. With other statements, the dilemma was evident. For example, TutorX had borrowed one of its values from Airbnb: "Make space for introverts." We could easily imagine dilemmas that this would address, such as "If my two smart, outspoken colleagues are dominating the conversation while others are sitting quietly, should I interrupt to ask the quieter colleagues to contribute, or let them remain silent since they might have nothing to say?" Because the statement was useful in guiding employee behavior in such a situation, TutorX kept it. In some cases, small wording changes yielded credible dilemmas. For instance, TutorX changed "We do it for the students" to "We put the needs of the students before the needs of the tutor," turning an abstract statement into a practical resolution for real-life dilemmas.

3. Paint Your Culture in Full Color

Once you have identified a clear set of values and dilemma-tested them, articulate your desired culture using concrete, colorful images to get the values to stick. Research on the picture superiority effect (PSE) shows that images lodge themselves in our memories in a way abstract words don't. If I ask you to remember the words "justice" and "pineapple," you are more likely to remember "pineapple." If I tell you that the pineapple is the size and texture of a groundhog covered in icicles, it lodges indelibly in your memory.

Consider Amazon's "two-pizza rule," which states that teams should not be made up of more people than two pizzas can feed. The image of 24 teammates fighting for a slice of pepperoni is hard to forget. More colorful still is Airbnb's "Elephants, dead fish, and vomit," which states that leaders should transparently address the things everyone is aware of but no one dares mention, the unpleasant events that are starting to stink, and the frustrating feelings people need to get out of their system. Amazon could have said, "We value small teams," and Airbnb, "We practice transparency," but neither would have the same behavioral impact.

Another way to put color into your organizational culture is to articulate it in an edgy, counterintuitive way. Be provocative, and your employees will remember. Netflix describes its culture in unforgettable statements like "Adequate performance gets a generous severance" and "Don't seek to please your boss, seek to do what's right for the company." With the latter, Netflix could have just said, "Do what's right for the business," but no one would have taken notice. The counterintuitive "Don't seek to please your boss" stops employees in their tracks and forces them to make each decision with the good of the company foremost in mind.

4. Hire the Right People, and They Will Build the Right Culture

"Garbage in, garbage out" is a computer science concept that states that if you don't have the right input data, the output will be rubbish no matter how good the programming. The concept also applies to your workforce. This is not to say that employees who are a bad fit are trash, of course. But if you hire people whose personalities don't align with your culture, no matter what else you get right, you are unlikely to get the desired behavior.

When defining company culture, first tackle whom you will hire. One company that has done this well is Patagonia. This

paragraph, clipped from its culture page (edited for length), demonstrates how to steer managers toward right-fit hiring decisions:

> *Patagonia doesn't advertise in the* Wall Street Journal
> *or hire corporate headhunters to find employees. We tap
> an informal network of friends and business associates—
> people who love to spend as much time as possible in the
> mountains or the wild. We are, after all, an outdoor com-
> pany. We would not staff our trade show booth with a
> bunch of out-of-shape guys wearing white shirts and ties
> any more than doctors would let their receptionists smoke
> in the office. We seek out "dirtbags" who feel more at home
> in a base camp or on the river than they do in the office. All
> the better if they have excellent qualifications, but we'll
> take a risk on an itinerant rock climber over a run-of-the-
> mill MBA.*

Those sentences are jam-packed with resolutions to hiring
dilemmas. Should I hire someone with technical expertise who
doesn't like to sleep in a tent? No. Should I take a chance on a
mountain biker who may not have the right technical experience? Yes. Should I pay a headhunter to find job candidates or
go through employee referrals? The latter.

Next look at whom you will fire. In an ideal world, once you
find your right-fit candidates, each will blossom into the employee of your dreams. Reality is more complicated. Some of
your hires will exceed your expectations; others will disappoint.
How your culture deals with those situations is as important as
whom you hire in the first place.

Would you like your company to have a family ethos where
people are confident in their job security? As one CEO said to

me, "Any kind, hardworking person will be nurtured here and rewarded with company loyalty." Or would you prefer to be more like an Olympic team? The founder and CEO of Shopify, Tobias Lütke, wrote in a letter to employees (edited for length): "Shopify is not a family. You are born into a family. They can't un-family you. The danger of 'family thinking' is that it becomes incredibly hard to let poor performers go. Shopify is a team."

If Shopify doesn't sound like the most comfortable place to work, consider a second part of its culture—typified by what I call the Bernard dilemma. Bernard is an extremely talented employee with a rare skill set that is essential to the business. He's innovative and gets things done. He is also arrogant, sarcastic, and a poor listener. You've provided him feedback and coaching. No change. Will you fire Bernard?

For companies like Shopify, the biggest risk is not that Bernard will upset his teammates. It is that one Bernard will turn into a company of Bernards. On a biological level, humans are programmed to mimic one another's behavior. We have neurons that fire when we watch another person, encouraging us to empathize and identify with that person. That's what makes bad behavior so contagious. For example, research by Will Felps of the University of New South Wales showed that when one team member behaves like a jerk, saying things like "You've got to be kidding me" or "Clearly, you've never taken a business class before," others become abrasive or obnoxious. The individual's personality becomes the group's culture.

Of course, some companies prize skill and talent above all other qualities and will take the antagonistic superstar over the kind, average worker every time. But Lütke makes it crystal clear what he wants his managers to remember when facing the Bernard dilemma: "Slack trolling, victimhood thinking, us-versus-them divisiveness, and zero-sum thinking must be seen for the threat they are." Netflix resolves the dilemma more simply, stating, "No brilliant jerks; the cost to teamwork is just too high."

5. Make Sure That Culture Drives Strategy

Many companies define their culture by focusing on employee attitudes. Witness the previously mentioned "We care" and "What you do matters" statements. Attitude is critical, and you should address it. But what's most important is to identify your strategic objective—whether it is to reduce costs, minimize business complexity, or scale up through mergers—and use dilemmas to ensure that your employees understand what decisions they should be making to move the business in the right direction.

If, for example, you seek to move from a culture of error elimination, consistency, and replicability (popular during the industrial era) to a culture of adaptability, innovation, and empowerment (increasingly necessary in the digital age), you will need dilemmas that encourage your managers to change direction quickly, remove bureaucratic processes, and take risks in the pursuit of fresh ideas.

Take the marketing software company HubSpot. It's culture brief states: "We are adaptable, constantly changing, lifelong learners." It then presents a hiring scenario that brings the value to life:

> *What about good people who just want stability and predictability? They may do good work, but they most likely won't be happy here.*

Any employee faced with the decision "Should I hire a highly talented employee who's seeking stability and predictability?" knows which way to lean: Don't make the hire.

Here's another example I've tested in my own research.

Dilemma

A member of your marketing team, Sheila, comes to you with a proposal she is passionate about. She's got a fresh (and expensive) idea for how to move the business forward. She has done her homework and thought through the risks and costs carefully. But you (Sheila's boss) think this project will fail. What will you do?

Option A: Reject the proposal and lean toward error prevention. As a manager your job is to use company resources wisely. Letting your employees invest in projects you think will flop would put those resources at risk. If Sheila can't convince you, it's not a good enough idea. You tell her (as kindly as possible), "Not this time."

Option B: Give the green light and lean toward innovation. You know that innovation involves trial and error. You want your talented employees to be empowered to try creative ideas they believe in. You've been wrong before. If the initiative fails, you will learn. You finance the project and shuffle work around. Sheila can get started.

About 68% of the managers I've questioned choose A. The industrial era powered the world's most successful economies for some 200 years, so it's no surprise that most of us are obsessed with eliminating error. And if you're running a nuclear reactor or manufacturing pharmaceutical drugs, you very well should be: A mistake may lead to loss of life. But in other realms, innovation is more important than efficiency or avoiding mistakes. The HubSpot and Sheila dilemmas provide managers with useful guidance in hiring the right people and then giving them the freedom to invest in fresh ideas. Sometimes ideas you are skeptical of will fail, and everyone will learn. But other times those ideas will pan out, and innovation will happen.

6. Don't Be a Purist

Of course, there will be times when the culture you've articulated should not (or cannot) be followed. When you debate your organizational culture, also identify dilemmas in which your stated values do *not* apply. Be bold and push the culture to the limit, but also define which situations are over the limit.

Imagine, for example, that "transparency" is a driving element of your culture. You've been sharing all kinds of information, telling your employees things leaders usually keep under wraps, and you've articulated a set of dilemmas that ensure that your managers know they should do the same. Yet you just fired your COO and feel that the circumstances should be kept private: Your lovable, hardworking second-in-command is an alcoholic, and his addiction was hurting the company. You seek to be transparent but feel it would be unfair to the COO to share this information. Transparency has come into tension with individual privacy, and privacy has won.

I came across a similar tension during my research at Netflix. Reed Hastings told me, "For our employees, transparency has become the biggest symbol of how much we trust them to act responsibly." Netflix took transparency so far that it shared quarterly financials with managers before the numbers were reported to Wall Street—something that almost no other publicly traded company was doing and that many onlookers saw as reckless.

Yet, even for this startlingly transparent company there was a limit. For Hastings the ultimate step was to allow employees to see everyone's compensation packages. He believed that salary transparency would encourage managers to think deeply about what they paid each employee while stamping out pay discrimination. By 2012 all vice presidents and above could see one another's pay, and in 2017 this was extended to directors and above (about 12% of the company). Hastings wanted the rule to apply to all employees.

But managers pushed back. As one director put it: "I look at people, and I see their salary flashing over their head. Olivia Kruger, $350,000; Howard Conner, $195,000." (These are not real names.) Another explained, "This is my private information. It's not OK for my manager to show my medical records to the team, nor is it OK to tell my colleagues how much money I'm making." A vote in the spring of 2018 showed that more than 80% of Netflix managers opposed sharing compensation information with all employees. Again, transparency came into tension with individual privacy, and privacy won.

While your culture should drive decision-making throughout the organization, consider it a North Star, not a straitjacket. As you identify which dilemmas will drive decision-making throughout the company, also consider the situations in which your culture as articulated would not apply. Clarify those limits explicitly. For the alcoholic ex-COO, you could tell your staff, "I feel Gerald's individual privacy trumps transparency. Gerald has left. We all love him. I don't feel comfortable saying more."

. . .

In the simplest terms, culture is the personality of a group. In the same way that you can describe an individual's personality ("Sandra is energetic, optimistic, and prone to errors and has a thousand fresh ideas") you can also describe a group's culture ("In this company, people are formal, quiet, and incredibly efficient and speak very directly to one another"). Although each individual in every group is different, the group culture influences the behavior of the individuals.

After you've taken pains to articulate your culture using colorful and actionable dilemmas, make sure that your top people are leading by example. If you tell your workforce, "No brilliant jerks," but have three Bernards on your executive team, your employees will see that the culture statements mean little, and no one will follow them. If you want your culture to take root, leadership must be the first to model it. In this case, there is no dilemma.

Originally published in July–August 2024. Reprint R2404C

5

Why Leadership Teams Fail

by Thomas Keil and Marianna Zangrillo

n their pursuit of strong performance, CEOs and executives often overlook a critical factor in organizational success: the health of their leadership team. That's a big problem, because a dysfunctional team can become a serious drag on strategy execution and erode morale. Not only that, the health of a senior team can make or break a CEO's tenure.

To learn more about what kinds of problems affect leadership teams and how leaders can solve them, we recently interviewed more than 100 CEOs and senior executives as part of a multiyear research program. What we encountered in the process was a recurrent narrative of dissatisfaction and disappointment.

Many of the leaders, after requesting anonymity, told us that their teams had so many internal problems that they were often unable to work together effectively. "When I arrived as CEO," one of them told us when we were researching our book

The Next Leadership Team, "there was an extremely dysfunctional team. There was almost no communication within the team, the communication with the board didn't reflect reality, and communication with the management levels below was completely absent. The people on the team simply didn't like working with each other."

For good reason, most CEOs don't like to talk publicly about problems on their leadership teams. But our research suggests that dysfunction is quite common. Instead of working together to advance their company's interests, many teams procrastinate, engage in political infighting, get mired in unproductive debates, let themselves be overtaken by complacency, and more. The companies they're supposed to be leading suffer as a result.

Every senior leadership team will have its own unique dynamic, of course, but our research revealed some recurring patterns. In this article, we'll introduce a typology of the common types of dysfunction that leadership teams fall into, and we'll offer remedies designed to help leaders address their team's specific problems and move toward alignment and high performance.

Shark Tanks, Petting Zoos, and Mediocracies

Leadership teams tend to exhibit one of three main patterns of dysfunction. The first, characterized by infighting and political maneuvering, we call a shark tank. The second, characterized by conflict avoidance and an overemphasis on collaboration, we call a petting zoo. And the third, characterized by complacency, a lack of competence, and an unhealthy focus on past success, we call a mediocracy. All three negatively affect team and corporate performance and can be equally disruptive.

Idea in Brief

The Problem

In pursuit of strong performance, CEOs often overlook a critical factor in organizational success: the health of their leadership team. That's a big problem, because a dysfunctional team can be a serious drag on strategy execution.

The Root Cause

There are three main patterns of dysfunction in leadership teams: the *shark tank*, characterized by infighting and political maneuvering; the *petting zoo*, characterized by conflict avoidance and an overemphasis on collaboration; and the *mediocracy*, characterized by complacency, a lack of competence, and an unhealthy focus on past success.

The Solution

By understanding and diagnosing these patterns of dysfunction, leadership teams can take a targeted approach to addressing them, which can lead to better strategy execution, higher morale, and overall organizational success.

The shark tank

Only highly ambitious leaders make it to the top team, and it's inevitable that they will compete with one another—to promote their ideas, gain access to scarce resources, or win promotions. Within limits, this is healthy and important, because competition fosters innovation and drives results. But unconstrained it can lead to a self-serving, destructive feeding frenzy in which meetings become battlegrounds for personal agendas, decisions are made through power struggles rather than open discussion, and teams have difficulty coming to consensus and executing on strategic initiatives. Such is life in the shark tank.

Consider the example of a Swiss bank that we studied. After a new CEO was hired, industry analysts and the press voiced criticism of the appointment. Before long some members of the leadership team took advantage of that criticism to gun for the CEO position themselves. These executives started bad-mouthing the CEO internally, slowed down the implementation of core projects that he had launched, fought with one another over projects and responsibilities, and even leaked confidential information to the press that portrayed the CEO and other potential contenders for his job in a negative light. This behavior damaged team morale and hindered the bank's ability to implement critical projects aimed at improving profitability and competitiveness. The situation became so dire that the board chair had to intervene and actively and publicly support the CEO to end speculation about a replacement.

Why do leadership teams become shark tanks? Often, our research suggests, it's because the CEO or the executive leading the team fails to provide clear direction, set boundaries, and reign in incipient aggressive behaviors among team members. Even a single rogue member who makes unchecked self-serving moves can force others to abandon their collaborative ethic, undermining morale and team effectiveness.

Leaders should be on the lookout for several signs that their team of competitive executives is at risk of devolving into a shark tank. Members might start approaching the CEO one-on-one to discuss topics that should be discussed in team meetings. Or they might start negotiating among themselves or engaging in power struggles outside of meetings, avoiding group discussion and debate on key decisions. Another warning sign is when decision-making erupts into shouting matches or when even relatively straightforward decisions turn into tug-of-war contests. Executives might continue to question and criticize plans after they've been made or resist implementing them unless forced to do so. They might begin to bad-mouth one another and form alliances against rivals, prioritizing personal gain over the collective good.

The petting zoo

The second pattern of dysfunction involves a misguidedly deferential approach to cooperation. Like competition, cooperation is essential to a healthy team—but when members of a leadership team sacrifice vigorous debate for a facade of harmony, organizational performance suffers.

Here's what team members stuck in the petting zoo have forgotten: Executive work is by nature a contact sport. The problems that top teams face rarely have an obvious solution; that's why they haven't been solved at lower levels of the organization. To address the complicated problems they're presented with, the members of a leadership team have to spar actively. They must challenge one another's ideas, question assumptions, and push back in debates. Even as they move collaboratively toward a shared goal, they are propelled by the forces of conflict, competition, and ambition. When these forces fade away, what's left is a petting zoo, in which an atmosphere of ineffectual niceness reigns. Everybody shies away from confrontation, meetings become echo chambers, ideas go unchallenged, and decisions are made without sufficient critical evaluation. As a result, teams uncover few opportunities for innovation, renewal, and growth.

A large European services company we studied exemplified this kind of dysfunction. The leadership team had been working together for many years and operated with a strong sense of camaraderie. Leaders had their own areas of responsibility, but all decisions were made by consensus. What's not to like?

A lot, as it turns out. During team meetings, there was little to no debate, team members automatically approved one another's proposals, and performance issues rarely were discussed openly, to avoid putting any individual leader on the spot. Team members were reluctant to challenge the status quo or hold one another accountable for failures, because they worried about disrupting the harmony of the team. This lack of candor and constructive criticism prevented the team from identifying and addressing critical problems, and the company found itself unable to meet its goals for growth and profitability.

Given how ambitious and competitive the members of most leadership teams are, why do some become petting zoos? Often, it's because the team leader has put an inordinate amount of emphasis on collaboration. Mutual trust and openness—key ingredients in collaboration—require a significant degree of vulnerability. Team members who actively challenge and confront their colleagues can be misunderstood as using that vulnerability to serve their own ends—even if they're pushing back for the good of the team. Sometimes a quid pro quo is at work too: Team members may agree not to invade one another's territory, engaging in a form of mutual forbearance that benefits each person individually but hurts the team's performance as a whole.

It's not all that easy to detect when a team starts to become a petting zoo, because the changes happen gradually and don't involve open conflict. On the surface, the leadership team may appear to be working together smoothly. The signs to look for are muted discussions, a lack of emotional intensity, and little robust debate. Sometimes the leadership team simply isn't willing—or able—to have a good fight to get to the best solution. Instead of putting issues on the table, the executives may engage in performance theater, focusing on positive news and downplaying problems. You may also notice members of the team horse-trading over projects and decisions in offline discussions so that they can avoid conflict during meetings.

The mediocracy

While the first two patterns of dysfunction emerge from an overemphasis on either competition or collaboration, the third pattern emerges when neither competition nor collaboration is emphasized enough. Team members lack the skills or motivation needed to drive individual unit performance; at the same time, there is little collaborative spirit on the team. The executives operate in silos, hindering synergy and leading to duplicated efforts and missed opportunities.

One CEO we interviewed recalled what he had encountered after taking the helm at a European professional services firm that was experiencing a period of stagnation. At the outset of his tenure, he undertook a three-month investigation of the leadership team—and discovered that it had become a mediocracy. "The team was really not fit for the purpose," he told us. "The individuals were not strong enough. They didn't have the competencies to run a scalable organization. More fundamentally, I felt that they were not working together as a team and didn't have a sense of corporate purpose. The word did not even exist in their vocabulary."

In mediocracies, there's a mismatch between what a team needs to do and what it is able to do. Long periods of success are sometimes to blame: Instead of challenging themselves and developing plans to meet the demands of the future, teams become complacent, fixate on past glories, and develop a harmful preference for the status quo. At other times, the source of the problem is a leader who allows the team to divide into two groups—one that prefers competition and another that prefers collaboration.

Mediocracies can also emerge when leaders fail to adjust to changing situations. Teams that function well in a stable environment may not be equipped to cope during economic crises, and those that are ideal for leading a turnaround may not be able to steer steady growth.

Reversing Course

If you detect any of these warning signs, you'll have to figure out how to get your team back on the path to high performance. How you do that depends on which kind of dysfunction you're dealing with.

From shark tank to team of stars

Conflict is everywhere in a shark tank, and the only way to settle things down is to locate the source—which often will turn out to be just one or two people who are engaging in self-serving behaviors that turn collaboration into cutthroat competition. If you discover that this is the case, you'll need to confront the individuals and make them aware of the effects of their behavior. You can start by giving them direction and offering coaching, but if they aren't willing or able to work with you on changing their behavior, you may simply need to remove them from the team. This can feel wrong if they're high performers, but given the detrimental effect that they are having on the whole team, it will be the right move in the long run—and the sooner you make it, the better.

That's what Adel Al-Saleh did at T-Systems, a division of Deutsche Telekom. Not long after starting as CEO, he tried to get his top team to work more collaboratively but found that some of his executives were openly resisting his efforts, with predictably disruptive results. So he removed them. This had a calming effect and enabled the team to do its work more productively.

If you want to not only control but also prevent shark-tank behaviors, you'll need to clearly define for your team what behaviors are desirable, acceptable, and unacceptable. Leaders of senior teams do this far too infrequently, but we have come across some who have adopted effective approaches. Morten Wierod, the CEO of ABB, a Swiss-Swedish multinational, explicitly discusses the expected behaviors with every person who joins his leadership team. Some CEOs and executives tie compensation to how well team members meet expectations and how productively they work together on key projects. For instance, John Hinshaw, the COO at the banking giant HSBC, uses 360-degree reviews to ensure that his team members' behaviors align with defined norms.

Role modeling is vital for driving behavioral change. When you engage in shark-tank behaviors yourself, you're obviously setting an example for the team. So carefully analyze your interactions with your team and adopt a deliberate approach to modeling desirable behaviors. When we asked Greg Poux-Guillaume, the CEO of the Dutch chemicals company AkzoNobel, how he avoids overly competitive behavior, he told us, "I try not to use information in tactical ways. I give everybody the same information. And I filter very little. That takes a lot of politics out of the team." In doing so, he is signaling that he endorses open and collaborative behaviors.

Providing regular feedback is also important in defusing rampant competition. Once you've made clear which behaviors are desirable—and you're modeling those behaviors yourself—you need to provide positive reinforcement to those who engage in them, and negative reinforcement to those who don't. Sara

Mella, the head of personal banking at Nordea, the largest bank in the Nordic region, methodically identifies the people who consistently engage in healthy debate and prioritize team goals over personal gain. She then encourages them to steer the team more, thereby gradually removing herself from the process and institutionalizing the behaviors.

From petting zoo to synergistic team

Changing behaviors in a petting zoo requires a different approach from what's required in a shark tank: You need to encourage more conflict among members of the leadership team, in the form of constructively critical debate. But you'll only be able to manage that if you can first create a foundation of trust and psychological safety. Everybody on the team must feel comfortable bringing problems to the table without worrying about how other team members or the CEO might react or even exploit the situation.

One way to help your team engage productively in difficult conversations is to ensure that good data is available to everybody. That helps root debate in fact, not opinion. One CEO we interviewed told us that when he began working with his leadership team, none of the unit or functional heads presented detailed operational, sales, and profitability data at meetings, which made it difficult for the senior team to neutrally evaluate performance and identify problems. So as a first step the CEO introduced monthly review meetings and insisted that detailed data be shared before each meeting. This allowed everybody to focus on analyzing and discussing the numbers in a neutral, data-driven way. Team members could raise questions for discussion or debate without seeming to attack one another personally.

Another way to counter the petting-zoo mentality is to monitor and improve the quality of the discussion that you and your team engage in. "Initially," Mario Greco, the CEO of Zurich Insurance, told us, "people did not want to talk openly. Everybody had their defenses, and people would not automatically speak up and discuss. Some would even bring consultants to our meetings." To address that problem, Greco shifted the focus of executive meetings from questions of policies and procedures to the interpretation of purpose and principles. During the biweekly executive committee meetings, he carefully followed how much discussion was happening, how many people were speaking up and raising issues or challenging colleagues, and how accepting team members were of being challenged by colleagues. These meetings, Greco said, have become a way for him to regularly take a temperature check of how well the team is functioning.

More debate, of course, can mean less consensus in the decision-making process. To members of a petting zoo, that can feel all wrong—but it's not. It's the job of a company's top managers to discuss, debate, and disagree, and it's the job of a leader to preside over the process, facilitating decision-making and acting as a tiebreaker when no clear consensus emerges.

From mediocracy to a set of high performers

If you find that most of your leaders are ill-suited for their roles or not up to the task, you may need to significantly remake your team. That's what Jonathan Lewis did when he took over the CEO role at Capita, a UK-based business-process services provider, in 2017. He removed everybody from the team and hired new executives on the basis of not only their management skills but also how well they aligned with the purpose, values, and strategic commitments he had defined for the company. With the new team in place, Lewis was able to completely rebuild the company during the global pandemic, which hit its customer-facing business hard. He increased the company's focus on its customers, improved its public image and Net Promoter Scores, and turned around financial performance.

In rebuilding your team, you'll need to strike the right balance between competition and collaboration, which means hiring people whose talents and styles are different but complementary. Dave Fredrickson, the executive vice president in charge of the oncology business unit at AstraZeneca, prioritizes this idea of balance when he thinks about the makeup of his team. "I want to have planners and dreamers," he said, "mixed with hard-nosed deliverers." He added that he considers it vital to set clear behavioral expectations. He tells everybody that at times natural collaborators will need to act competitively, and at times natural competitors will need to act collaboratively. So he leads by example, modeling the mode of behavior that's most desirable in a given situation.

When mixing different types of personalities, it can be helpful to define in which domains collaborative or competitive behaviors should dominate. For instance, Erwin Mayr, the CEO of Wieland Group, a global leader in copper products, has made clear to his team that in some domains (such as IT, sustainability, and procurement), he expects a focus on coordination and collaborative problem-solving, whereas in others (such as product portfolio and pricing decisions in individual markets), he feels a more competitive approach is called for—one that gives each business unit decision-making freedom. This approach helps avoid confusion and creates much greater accountability among members of the team.

The Steps to High-Performing Teams

Our research suggests that it's often a lack of clarity—strategic, operational, and behavioral—that paves the way for leadership-team dysfunction. Without clearly defined expectations, team members struggle to understand their roles and how their efforts contribute to the bigger picture.

No matter what kind of dysfunction a company may need to address, there are several general steps that all leaders should take to ensure the health of their teams:

Develop a clear vision and purpose. Articulate a compelling vision for your tenure that provides a road map for decision-making and creates a sense of shared purpose.

Focus on alignment. Populate your team with people whose skills and temperament align with your vision and purpose. Make sure they possess backgrounds, experiences, and strengths that will contribute to the team's collective success.

Outline responsibilities. Clearly define goals, roles, and decision-making authority in order to avoid confusion and wasted effort.

Establish behavioral norms. Make clear what norms you expect your team to observe, and encourage members to do so through coaching, role modeling, and giving individual and team feedback.

. . .

Admittedly, addressing dysfunction on your leadership team can be fraught, because it requires making hard choices about the people you work most closely with. But for that reason, it's critical that you set aside your preferences and opinions and follow the kind of analytical approach that we recommend in this article—first diagnosing which specific pattern of dysfunction afflicts your team and then adopting a targeted approach to address it. Only then will you be able to lead a team that is capable of lifting your organization to a new performance level.

Originally published in September–October 2024. Reprint S24052

6

How to Assess True Macroeconomic Risk

by Philipp Carlsson-Szlezak and Paul Swartz

O ver the past five years corporate leaders and investors have had to digest a rapid succession of macroeconomic shocks, crises—and false alarms. In 2020, when the pandemic delivered an intense recession, leaders were told it would be worse than 2008 and potentially as bad as the Great Depression. Instead a fast and strong recovery unfolded. In 2021, when supply bottlenecks and strong demand sent prices soaring, a common view was that runaway inflation would take us back to the ugly 1970s. Instead inflation fell from 9.1% to just above 3% in a year. In 2022, when U.S. interest rates climbed, a cascade of emerging-market defaults were predicted—but they didn't materialize. Also in 2022, and again in 2023, public discourse cast an imminent recession as "inevitable." Instead a resilient U.S. economy not only defied the doomsayers but delivered strong growth.

For executives and investors such whiplash comes with two types of costs: financial and organizational. Consider the financial cost to automakers that reduced their semiconductor orders in 2020 because they misread the Covid-19 recession as a protracted economic depression. That meant they missed out on sales during the roaring recovery. And leaders can lose the trust of their organizations if they overreact to false alarms with abrupt reversals in strategy, operations, and communications. Clearly, getting the macro call right really matters.

The current turmoil is particularly painful because it comes after 40 years of relative calm. Many executives built their careers and businesses with powerful structural winds at their backs. In the real economy, volatility moderated and cycles grew longer. In the financial realm, inflation fell gradually for decades and pulled interest rates down with it. Around the world, a convergence of institutional arrangements encouraged executives to build a global web of value chains. Yes, setbacks occurred, chief among them the global financial crisis of 2008. Nonetheless, for most of the past few decades, macroeconomic risks have taken a back seat in boardrooms.

Today faith in such stability has been shaken. Shocks and crises are back—but as we have shown, so are false alarms. Without an understanding of the forces that drive disruptions, executives will have a hard time keeping their balance as economic conditions, and the narratives around them, seesaw violently. Shocks and crises pose a real threat, but so does overreaction to them. And for every true crisis there are many false alarms. Understanding macroeconomic risk—the potential for negative or positive change, both cyclical and

Idea in Brief

The Situation

After decades of relative calm, macroeconomic shocks and crises are dominating headlines and complicating corporate strategy. Unfortunately, the field of macroeconomics is of little help. If anything, it has contributed to the problem, by inviting knee-jerk and too confident reactions to volatile dataflow.

Why It Persists

No economic model succeeded in predicting the shocks of the past five years while avoiding the false alarms. Models and their forecasts are least reliable when they are most needed: in times of crisis. But when the economy is in free fall, executives are understandably desperate for guidance as to what might happen next.

The Solution

In this article the authors outline how leaders can cultivate their judgment—and use it to see past negative headlines, to draw on diverse sources, to identify key causal narratives, and ultimately to make better calls.

structural—is essential to responding to these threats with rational optimism.

In this article we will outline how leaders can better discern which risks are genuine. We will also sketch the landscape of real, financial, and global economic risks they face and demonstrate how risks in each category can be approached. Understanding risk is not about building the right model—no matter what many economists will tell you. To be sure, perfect foresight is impossible even if we look beyond the confines of modeling. But executives can cultivate their judgment—and use it to see past the headlines, to identify key causal narratives, and ultimately to make better calls.

Reclaiming Macroeconomic Judgment

For all its scientific veneer and Greek-letter equations, the discipline of macroeconomics offers no precise instruments for business leaders to rely on. No economic model succeeded in predicting the shocks of the past five years while avoiding the false alarms. If anything, the field contributed to the problem, by inviting knee-jerk and too-confident reactions to volatile dataflow.

Still, by embracing three analytical habits that can result in better macroeconomic judgment, leaders stood a fair chance of recognizing the false alarms mentioned above. The key is an approach that values contextual flexibility over theoretical rigidity, rational optimism over doom mongering, and judgment over prediction.

Let go of master-model mentality

No single theory or approach can provide a consistently accurate economic forecast. The track record of such forecasting is so poor that economic models are rarely a source of insight and often one of false alarms. Surprisingly, the common belief that sophisticated models yield precise and useful answers has persisted even as misguided predictions have piled up.

Models are unreliable because macroeconomic relationships are context-dependent and use small sample sizes. For instance, each recession in the United States since World War II was the result of a highly idiosyncratic constellation of drivers, and there were only 12 of them. Thus supposedly scientific recession modeling is often remarkably unscientific.

That criticism isn't new. More than a century ago the economist Ludwig von Mises railed against the "fallaciousness" of assuming "constant relations" in economics. John Maynard Keynes drew a distinction from the natural sciences by saying that economics is "not constant through time." And Friedrich Hayek thought it an "outright error" that economics tries to "imitate . . . the brilliantly successful natural sciences." But instead of heeding such warnings, the discipline has added layer upon layer of scientific veneer that is of little use to leaders who must navigate volatility in the real world.

Compounding this problem is the fact that models and their forecasts are least reliable when they are most needed: in times of crisis. When the economy is in free fall, executives are understandably desperate for guidance as to what might happen next. But by definition, crises generate extreme data points—so in situations where predictions would be most valuable, the models are asked to extrapolate beyond the data on which they were built.

The Covid pandemic illustrated this clearly. Several important indicators—including changes in GDP, consumption, imports, and unemployment—swung so dramatically that they were far outside the range of typical historical experience. (See the exhibit "The limits of models.") Take, for example, the monthly change in the U.S. unemployment rate: In 90% of the months over the past 70 years it has shifted up or down by just 0.3 percentage points or less. But in April 2020 it increased by 10.3 percentage points. The idea that a path to economic recovery could have been precisely modeled when the models had never before seen such shifts is laughable.

The limits of models

During Covid, beginning in 2020, economic indicators moved far outside the range of normal experience. This made forecasting models perform poorly. The data below shows the highs and lows in economic indicators during the pandemic and their 70-year pre-Covid range.

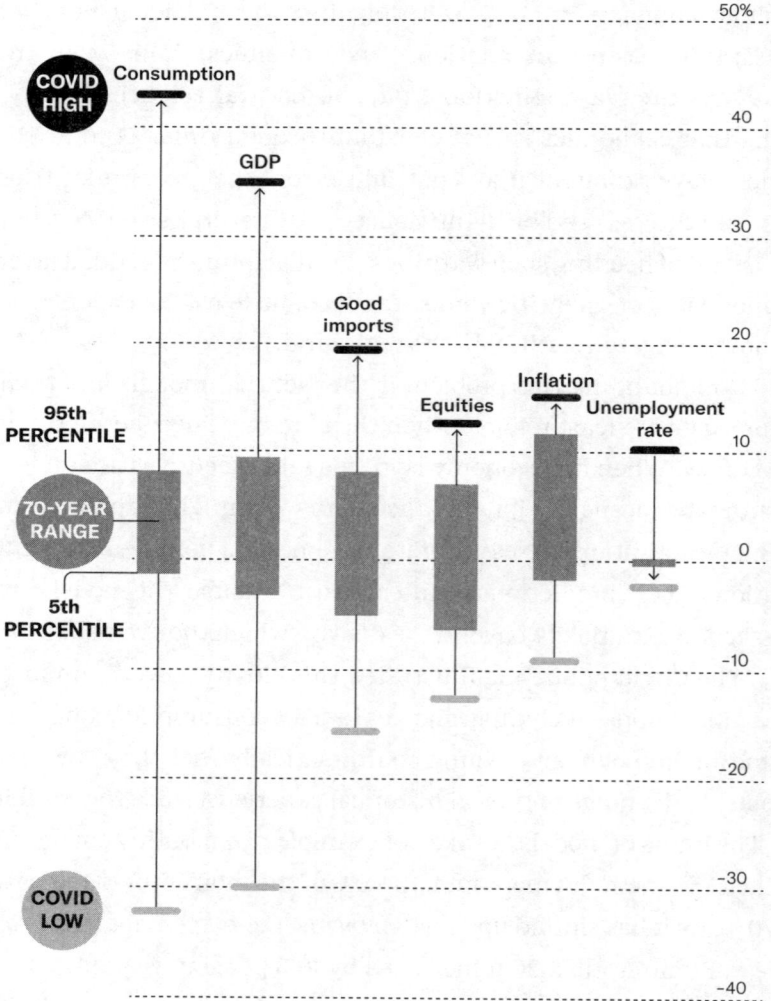

Note: The chart shows changes to economic indicators, not their levels. GDP and consumption (both real) are quarter-over-quarter annualized. Imports (real) are quarter-over-quarter. Equities (S&P 500) and inflation (CPI) are month-over-month; unemployment is month-over-month in percentage points; inflation (CPI) are month-over-month annualized. Data since 1950; 70-year range through 2019.

Source: BEA, BLS, S&P, analysis by BCG Center for Macroeconomics

Discount doom mongering

Leaders must contend with a constant drumbeat of headlines foretelling disaster. Why the negative bent? Simple: Doom sells. Economic and financial journalists rarely have an opportunity to write about sex, crime, or celebrities. Crises and collapse are reasonable substitutes in a competition to attract eyeballs and generate clicks. That is true across television, print, and online media. And even the most respectable outlets, along with pundits and commentators, reliably dial up negative coverage. Thus false alarms are amplified as the microphone is inevitably passed to the loudest pessimists in the room, who grab airtime by confidently portraying long-shot if valid risks from the edges of the risk distribution as being at its very center.

Public discourse does not hold the doomsayers accountable. Predicting the 2008 global financial crisis provided rich rewards for perennially bearish commentators—but looks less impressive considering that those same pundits predicted another dozen crises that somehow didn't materialize. A broken clock is right twice a day.

Without judgment of their own, executives have little to protect them from the pull of this negativity. Leaders need to choose their clicks wisely and remember who is speaking and from what perch. They don't have to follow every news cycle that spins the latest data point into a story of collapse. And they must be able to quickly calibrate the stories they do spend time on by asking, simply: *What would it take for this to happen?*

Practice judgment through economic eclecticism

There is an alternative to master models and doomscrolling. To stand a better chance of getting macroeconomics right, leaders must develop a situationally aware mindset that is focused on causal persuasiveness and coherence of narrative. Inputs to this sort of judgment should come not only from economics but also from adjacent (and far-flung) disciplines and methods. Sometimes frameworks help us understand risks; sometimes historical episodes are illuminating; sometimes even formal economic models can be useful. Narratives about how the system works matter and can be used to stress-test the bold claims in economic debate. And once it is understood that macroeconomics lacks the analytical elegance of, say, physics, leaders can more confidently bring in broader perspectives and methods. Macroeconomics is not best suited to be a soloist; it plays better as part of a band.

An eclectic approach is accessible to and appropriate for those with inquiring minds—a group that includes many business executives and investors. Equipped with curiosity and judgment, leaders should not be intimidated by number crunchers and model-wedded forecasters, whose grasp of risk and context may be far weaker than their own. Economic eclecticism doesn't seek to shut down debate the way model-generated "truths" do. It encourages rigorous argument, which is the cornerstone of good judgment.

Executives know that leadership is about navigating uncertainty. If the future were readily predictable, leading would be no more than execution. Assessing economic risks involves a combination of knowledge, skill, and experience—in a word, judgment.

Let's turn to specific demonstrations of eclectic judgment, looking at risks within the real, financial, and global domains.

The Real Economy: How to Avoid Falling for the Worst Cyclical Calls

The real economy concerns ups and downs in the production and consumption of goods and services, and it often dominates perceptions of the macroeconomic risk landscape. That is only natural: The ability to anticipate coming recessions or incipient recoveries is particularly valuable to executives.

But forecasting macro cycles remains fiendishly hard, as the pandemic illustrates. Why was the recovery from Covid predicted to be far worse than what followed the global financial crisis of 2008? Because cyclical models often anchor on the unemployment rate. After 2008 that rate rose to 10% and then took many years to come down. Thus in 2020, when unemployment spiked to near 15%, the models concluded that the recovery would be even more sluggish. Master-model thinking unwittingly and erroneously extrapolated from the shock's intensity to its legacy, feeding narratives of a "Greater Depression."

However, an eclectic approach showed early on that intensity and legacy are not causally linked. The long-term scarring of an economy—the cause of a poor recovery—requires that the economy's capacity (the supply side) be damaged. To leave scars like those of 2008, a crisis must cripple balance sheets, slow investment and the growth of capital stock, break the labor market, and collectively undermine productivity growth.

We can conceptualize the legacy of a crisis by distinguishing between recovering to the precrisis *trend of output* and recovering to the precrisis *growth rate*. After the global financial crisis, the United States eventually achieved a growth rate similar to the one prior to the crisis. But output never regained its precrisis trend. Too little investment occurred, and too many skills were lost, leaving a permanent scar on the economy's supply side and lowering the economy's future potential. Yet despite the far greater intensity of the Covid recession, the economy made a successful return to both output trend *and* growth rate. (See the exhibit "A better recovery.")

Could that "V-shaped" recovery have been foreseen? Even in March and April of 2020, when consensus suggested a lengthy recovery, it was possible to outline a narrative in which the recovery was full—as we did in "Understanding the Economic Shock of Coronavirus" (HBR.org, March 27, 2020). Of course, Covid's intensity had the *potential* to cripple balance sheets and degrade capital, labor, and productivity. But comparisons to either 2008 or the 1930s failed to look at a full range of drivers and ask: *What would it take?*

An eclectic (and rationally optimistic) view of the recovery focused on the many drivers of supply-side damage and the instruments to prevent it. Comparisons to 2008 failed to see that 2020 lacked an investment bubble, or leveraged balance sheets, or a rickety financial system—even if the later recession was more intense. And comparisons to the Great Depression lacked an appreciation of what delivered that catastrophe: persistent policy failure as those in charge stood by and watched the economy bleed out. During the pandemic, political interests in the United States aligned—despite extreme partisanship—to deliver "existential" stimulus.

No model or forecast could compete with an eclectic view of recovery potential, which was about so much more than macroeconomics. It required a reading of supply-side risks and policy instruments to offset them, of finance and the health of balance sheets, of crisis politics and the nature of stimulus, of history

A better recovery

After the global financial crisis, the growth rate recovered but output never returned to its precrisis trend. By contrast, the post-Covid economy quickly returned to old growth rates and trend.

Real GDP
US$(2012)

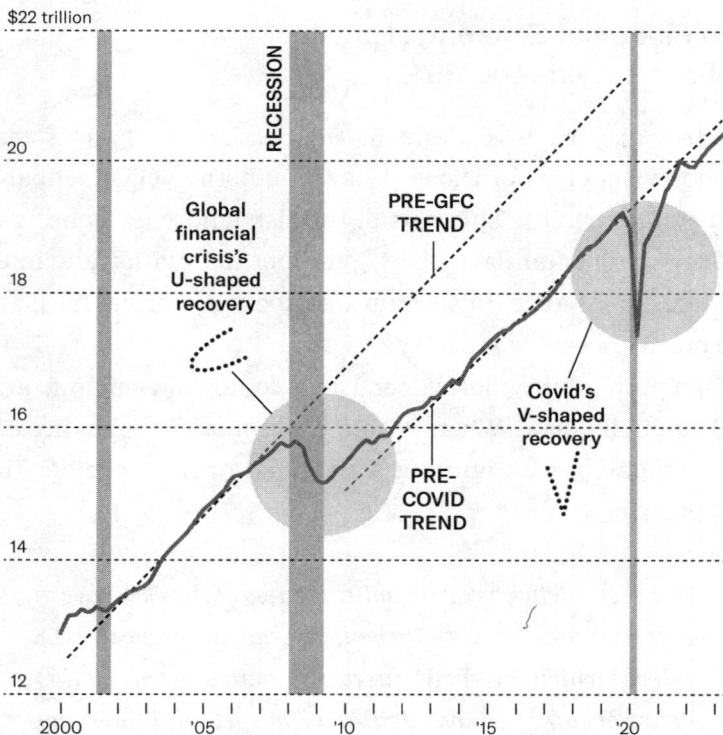

Note: Data through Q2 2023

Source: BEA, NBER, analysis by BCG Center for Macroeconomics

and structural changes since prior crises, and of the capacity for societal adaptation. In short, it required judgment. Even with a coherent narrative about drivers, it was not possible to deliver a precise forecast of recovery. But it *was* possible to deliver a rationally optimistic call that avoided doomsaying.

The Financial Economy: How to Calibrate Systemic Risk

Leaders may be less aware of financial risks than of real-economy shocks, but those risks bring both cyclical jeopardy and systemic peril. This part of the risk landscape contains a wide range of potential threats: gyrations in inflation and interest rates, a reliance on stimulus, a proclivity for bubbles, and the prevalence of debt.

One particularly thorny, persistent source of economic anxiety is public debt. When does a government's debt threaten its economy or risk igniting a financial crisis? Consider this perspective:

> With every deficit year the indebtedness of the U.S. government goes up, and with it the interest charges on the U.S. budget, which in turn raises the deficit even further. Sooner or later . . . confidence in America and the American dollar will be undermined—some observers consider this practically imminent.

Although this could have been written in 2024, Peter Drucker wrote it in 1986. In the nearly 40 years since then, the U.S. public debt has risen almost without pause while the value of the dollar has neared record highs in recent years. Rather than being a cause of crises, that debt has been a critical solution to them several times over, such as in 2008 and 2020. Meanwhile, Germany and other economies that put austerity above the use of debt have underperformed the United States.

Why, then, the existential angst? The perennial prediction of a U.S. debt crisis invariably anchors on debt *levels,* suggesting that some tipping point will trigger systemic unraveling. Influential economists, including Carmen Reinhart and Kenneth Rogoff, have worked to wrap this idea in scientific precision. Reinhart and Rogoff argued in 2010 that exceeding a debt-to-GDP ratio of 90% would lead to collapsing growth. Thresholds like that not only failed to predict debt problems but also fed into misguided post-2008 austerity narratives and spread unjustified gloom.

Executives looking at public debt to assess systemic risk—not just in the United States—should spend less time thinking about debt levels and more time thinking about interest rates versus growth rates. The interplay between those two determines an economy's ability to pay its debt. When the growth rate is higher than the interest rate, all the interest can be paid for with new debt without raising the debt-to-GDP ratio. But when the interest rate rises above the growth rate, the economy must set aside income just to keep the ratio stable.

Thus, calibrating the risk from public debt involves asking whether interest rates could durably rise above the growth rate of GDP. In the United States, although long-term interest rates are likely to be higher in the 2020s, it's difficult to see how they will be persistently above nominal growth. But even when growth drops below interest rates, it is not automatically "game over." It does, however, become costly and force trade-offs. Fiscal profligacy is always unwise.

The question of public debt demonstrates that executives must remain vigilant about economic models and doom mongering in the media when it comes to financial risk. Rather than anchoring on a clear but questionable metric (debt levels), an eclectic leader searches for key drivers, constructs narratives, and evaluates their coherence by drawing on a rich range of sources. In this case the key driver is the interplay of interest rate and growth rate—and the numerous factors that have a role in determining them.

The Global Economy: How to Navigate Divergence

Today geopolitics appears to occupy an ever-greater share of the risk landscape, which is particularly challenging because it was relatively calm for so long. A multidecade trend toward the global *convergence* of political, security, economic, and financial systems had made geopolitics all but irrelevant in macroeconomics. Now global *divergence* forces leaders to rapidly climb a risk-management learning curve. Surely geopolitical turmoil casts a shadow on the global economy.

But does it really? We cannot model the impact of geopolitics on the global economy with any real confidence. Not even the simple direction of the relationship (positive or negative) can be assumed.

Consider the two world wars. When World War I broke out, the stock market dropped 10% in three days and was subsequently closed down. When it reopened 136 days later, it was down another 20%. The fall captured a seemingly straightforward pass-through from geopolitics to economic impact.

Yet when World War II broke out, the U.S. stock market jumped 13%. This time a geopolitical calamity materially improved the economic backdrop in the United States. That's because World War II delivered an enormous demand boost to the U.S. economy, effectively (and finally) ending the Great Depression. Though the downside of geopolitical stress, crisis, and conflict is real and can be catastrophic, the ability to predict flashpoints or their knock-on effects remains poor. And even when a geopolitical outcome is accurately predicted, understanding its economic impact is an entirely different undertaking, as demonstrated previously.

The best way to navigate such uncertainty is by trying to predict not whether or when the gun will fire but how the bullet will ricochet through a complex maze of real, financial, and institutional channels. To begin with, the economic factor with the greatest impact may be the policy response rather than the geopolitical event itself. The big lift to the U.S. economy from WWII didn't come until the country's full mobilization after Pearl Harbor.

The present hears many echoes. The war in Ukraine has barely left a mark on the U.S. economy. The eurozone, much more directly exposed, escaped a downturn over the past two years, defying the commonplace extrapolation that this shock would lead to a recession. Similarly, multiple conflicts in the Middle East—as devastating as they've been for the economies in its midst—have left few marks on the global economy, because the linkages are few and the workarounds many. This is not calloused or nihilistic: Wars and geopolitical hostilities rightly dominate debate because of their devastating human toll—and because they can escalate. But that doesn't make economic doom mongering accurate. Leaders tasked with gauging the impact of geopolitical shocks on the macroeconomy need to dig deeper.

What can improve the odds of making the right call? Regarding the real economy, we should ask: *Will a geopolitical shock change spending power? Will it change the calculus of investment?* Regarding the financial economy: *Will geopolitics change credit creation or intermediation? Will it undermine or weaken companies' balance sheets?* And on the institutional front: *Will it change the explicit or implicit rules of the road?* This is just an abbreviated list, but it illustrates how context and reaction, rather than the shock itself, define the economic impact.

The Case for Rational Optimism

Our helicopter tour of real, financial, and global risks highlights pitfalls and opportunities for leaders, who can't rely on forecasts and the media to provide answers. As with every other aspect of leadership, they must ultimately exercise judgment.

Letting go of prescriptive models, actively leaning against the doomsaying slant in public discourse, and taking an eclectic perspective will give executives a better shot at calibrating macroeconomic risk—even if outcomes cannot consistently be predicted. Those who are willing to do this work will also discover a more optimistic take on the future. Despite the menacing landscape, we believe that an era of economic tightness should make executives feel upbeat about the prospects for the U.S. economy.

In the real economy, structurally tight labor markets will keep workers in short supply. That will push companies to invest and discover productivity gains in order to contain labor costs. Growth opportunities will outweigh growth risks in the years ahead. In the financial economy, tighter utilization of both labor and capital will deliver higher interest rates. Though they strain the economy and pose systemic risks, we see them as good on balance, because they lead to better capital allocation. And in the global economy, continued convergence would have been preferable, but divergence will also boost the U.S. economy in the years ahead: It will drive more capital expenditure in domestic manufacturing alongside strategic investment in other needs such as decarbonization and AI. New recessions will come, but they are unlikely to end the era of tightness.

The "dismal science" of economics and our clickbait culture of public discourse are a perfect match to fuel simplistic narratives of doom. To avoid false alarms and achieve a true assessment of macroeconomic risks, leaders should look past both to reclaim their own judgment.

Originally published in July–August 2024. Reprint R2404E

Five Ways to Ask Your Boss to Advocate for You

by Melody Wilding

Emily, a product manager at a video gaming company, had recently been tapped to lead a new AI work group. Incorporating machine learning into its game development was a major strategic direction for the firm, and she felt honored to spearhead such a crucial initiative. But colleagues from other departments were slow to respond to her emails, often missing meetings or deprioritizing AI-related tasks. She told me, "My boss keeps saying to give it time. That new projects take a while to gain traction." When Emily did manage to gather her stakeholders, she sensed a lack of urgency and buy-in. "They see this work group as just another burden," Emily said. "I know we'd move faster if there was more visible support from my boss and the rest of the leadership team."

Maybe you've been in Emily's shoes, wishing your manager would advocate for you, whether through the public endorsement of an idea, introductions to key stakeholders, publicizing team achievements, or positioning you as a subject-matter expert. Your leader's support can lend credibility, open doors, and rally resources in a way that's hard to do on your own—but it's often up to you to ask for it.

In an ideal world, higher-ups would instinctively and unquestioningly champion your efforts. But the truth is, your supervisor is busy juggling multiple priorities and your project may have slipped their mind. If they're new to their role, they might be hesitant to throw their weight around. In some cases, your boss may intentionally wait and see how you go about getting buy-in on your own. Most of the time, though, leaders simply don't recognize when their advocacy is needed, how impactful it can be, or what obstacles you're facing.

Regardless of the reason, waiting for support to magically materialize is a surefire way to aggravate yourself and potentially derail your project. So, how do you manage up and ask for the help you need? Here's how to convince those above you to champion your cause.

Highlight what's in it for them

Your boss, like everyone, is tuned into their personal "radio station," WII-FM (what's in it for me?). To gain their support, you need to broadcast on their frequency. In other words, connect your ask to how it not only meets your needs, but also aligns with their priorities.

Emily knew from past one-on-ones that her manager was concerned about efficiency and his own workload. So, she highlighted how increased visibility for the AI work group could speed up project timelines by reducing back-and-forth communication and limit the number of meetings he'd need to attend.

Idea in Brief

The Problem

Employees often struggle to get the support they need from their managers, especially when it comes to advocating for their projects or career advancement. Many leaders simply don't recognize when their advocacy is needed, how impactful it can be, or the obstacles employees are facing. This lack of advocacy can hinder progress and morale.

The Solution

Five strategies can effectively ask your boss for advocacy: highlighting what's in it for them, offering concrete suggestions for how to support you, giving your boss ready-made language they can share, implementing a regular win routine, and leveraging reciprocity.

The Benefits

By using these strategies, employees can gain more visible support from their bosses, leading to faster project progress, increased buy-in from colleagues, and overall career growth.

Offer specific ideas

Don't leave it to your leader to figure out how to support you. Instead, come prepared with concrete suggestions. Identify specific stakeholders, meetings, presentations, or company communications where your boss could advocate for your work. They're more likely to say yes because you've done the thinking for them—and it also shows your understanding of the organization's politics.

When Emily approached her manager, she pitched an idea: "What if you gave us a shout-out in the next all-hands meeting or in the company newsletter? I believe a mention from you would really highlight the importance of our work—especially since AI is a key focus area now—and would solidify my role as the group's leader."

Give your boss a spiel

By providing your boss with ready-made language they can share, you remove barriers to action and control the narrative, ensuring that your efforts are presented in the way you want them to be. For example, you might give your manager:

- Concise talking points about your project that they can easily incorporate into conversations or presentations

- A brief, polished script they could use to introduce you at company events or meetings

- Customizable email templates for connecting you with different stakeholders or promoting your work

- A set of frequently asked questions with clear, concise answers to help them field objections or defend your ideas to senior leadership

- Prewritten social media posts they can share on professional networks to highlight the progress or impact of your work

Implement a weekly win routine

Once a week or twice a month, send a brief, bulleted email to your boss highlighting your team's achievements, challenges you have overcome, and upcoming milestones. By doing so, you're handing them a neatly packaged "cheat sheet" of information they can use to impress their boss and peers. It's a win-win: your manager appears on top of things, and your hard work gets the spotlight it deserves.

This simple routine also gets you into the habit of articulating and documenting your achievements, which is a powerful way of boosting your confidence. Plus, when it's time for your performance review, you'll have concrete examples at your fingertips and won't have to scramble for data to make a case for resources or advancement.

Leverage reciprocity

The psychological principle of reciprocity says that when someone does something for us, we feel naturally inclined to return the favor. So, look for opportunities to highlight your boss's leadership, priorities, strengths, and successes. By showing that you value and promote their work, you make it more likely they'll do the same for you. This isn't meant to be a quid pro quo, but rather managing up in a supportive way that builds trust and goodwill.

Sincerity is key. Don't force praise where it doesn't fit naturally. Just be on the lookout for little moments to acknowledge your boss's ideas and contributions. This could be as simple as sending a quick note to thank them for their guidance on how to deliver tough feedback to an employee or being an active participant when they're leading a workshop.

Remember, your success at work goes beyond doing a great job. It relies on making sure your value is seen, understood, and appreciated. By taking the initiative to ask for and enable advocacy from your boss, you're taking control of your professional narrative.

Adapted from hbr.org, September 30, 2024. Reprint H08EPO

7

What Comes After DEI

by Lily Zheng

The need for more inclusive workplaces for all is undeniable—91% of workers have experienced discrimination related to race, gender, disability, age, or body size, according to a poll conducted by Monster, and 94% of workers care about feeling a sense of belonging at work, according to APA's 2023 Work in America Survey. But Pew research indicates that anti-DEI rhetoric and backlash has sunk support for diversity, equity, and inclusion (DEI) to a low of only 52% of American workers.

The predominant response to this backlash among practitioners I've talked to has been to largely continue with the status quo, rebrand the language as needed, and adhere to existing initiatives and programs under the DEI umbrella that remain legal until forced to do otherwise. Fewer practitioners—or employers—are considering whether DEI work itself has room to improve.

In this moment, leaders and practitioners invested in building healthier workplaces and societies for everyone have a once-in-a-generation opportunity to reimagine this work—not only to adapt to a new sociopolitical climate, but to let go of practices that have outlived their usefulness and refocus efforts on what works.

Decades of research show clear problems with status quo DEI. Despite their widespread prescription, DEI trainings often fail to change bias or reduce prejudice. Popular strategies for communicating the value of DEI can paradoxically both hurt marginalized communities *and* decrease leadership support for DEI. Common initiatives intended to create better workplaces for all might instead activate backlash, increase burnout, and fail to improve outcomes for underserved groups.

DEI needs a reset. People want more diverse, equitable, and inclusive workplaces, but the initiatives and approaches common to mainstream DEI are far from the only way to achieve them.

Drawing from research, conversations with colleagues, and my own work over the last decade as a DEI practitioner, I've developed a replacement that I call the FAIR framework. It's built around the core outcomes of fairness, access, inclusion, and representation that DEI was supposed to achieve for all, and it offers four principles to guide this work.

What Does a Better Model Look Like?

As I wrote in the hbr.org article "What Needs to Change About DEI—and What Doesn't," the mainstream DEI strategy adopted by many organizations—marked by jargon-heavy communication, siloed programming reliant on burned-out volunteers, one-off workshops utilizing outdated tactics like blame and shame, and little measurement or accountability—often created the appearance of progress at best and substantial backlash at worst.

Idea in Brief

The Problem

While backlash to diversity, equity, and inclusion (DEI) has challenged how many companies and practitioners approach creating more equitable workplaces, few have considered whether DEI work itself has room to improve.

The Solution

A new framework, built around the core outcomes of fairness, access, inclusion, and representation (FAIR) that DEI was supposed to achieve for all, offers a new direction. Instead of the performative, individual-centered, isolated, and zero-sum methods of the current mainstream approach, DEI work must evolve to become outcomes-based, systems-focused, coalition-driven, and win-win.

The Benefits

By emphasizing fairness in policies, broad accessibility, inclusive cultures, and trust-based representation, organizations can better address the needs of all employees and create meaningful, lasting change.

Leaders at the forefront of reimagining this work are using data to design interventions that measurably improve outcomes for all. They apply a change management approach to create impact at scale, improving personnel policies; hiring, promotion, and feedback processes; leadership incentives; and organizational culture and norms, rather than repeatedly seeking to "build awareness" without follow-up. They are building coalitions that engage everyone in the workplace as part of the solution, rather than looking to pin problems on one social identity group versus another. And they are communicating in ways that defuse defensiveness and threat by establishing the benefit of this work for everyone, rather than resorting to rhetoric that inflames intergroup hostility and polarization.

"I've been encouraged by data that show if you design for better processes, you don't always need to first get everyone on board," said Ruchika T. Malhotra, author of *Inclusion on Purpose*. "Actions most often change as a result of intentionally designed processes. For example, designing a more equitable hiring process actually benefits people of *all* backgrounds. But if people are resistant to the word 'equitable,' it shouldn't stop leaders from designing for better hiring outcomes using the same principles."

This development in the DEI space has been a slow-moving revolution resisted by leaders and practitioners more comfortable with the status quo. Now, DEI must adapt in exactly this way if it wants to survive. Instead of the performative, individual-centered, isolated, and zero-sum methods of the current mainstream approach, DEI work must evolve to become:

- *Outcomes-based*, focusing on measurable results like pay equity, physical and psychological safety, wellness, and promotion rates, rather than bandwagoning (and only budgeting for) a onetime training, posting on social media, or other behaviors that signal commitment without demonstrating results. Rather than gauge an employer by whether they have *committed* to progress, an outcomes-based approach requires us to gauge an employer by whether they have measurably *achieved* progress.

- *Systems-focused*, using change management to achieve healthier workplace systems—policies, processes, practices, and norms—rather than a "self-education" approach. For example, rather than ask every person to align their individual beliefs with an arbitrary standard of "inclusion," a systems-focused approach aims to achieve inclusion at scale by rewarding inclusive leaders, creating inclusive workplace processes, and normalizing expectations for inclusive behavior.

- *Coalition-driven*, focusing on engaging the wide range of people who stand to benefit from a healthier and fairer workplace, rather than limiting participation by identity or ideology. Rather than delegating the blame for a problem or the onus of problem-solving to small groups of employees, a coalition-building approach aims to engage everyone in taking responsibility and working together to find solutions that work for all, even if not everyone shares the same beliefs about the work.

- *Win-win*, focusing not only on creating better outcomes for all, but communicating the benefits of progress—even if it might look limited or localized at first—for everyone. A win-win approach intentionally aims to push back against the notion that progress could be zero sum: for example, rather than assuming that only women will be interested in challenging gender bias, a win-win approach might involve reaching out to people of all genders with the assumption that challenging gender biases benefits everyone.

How Can FAIR Succeed Where DEI Has Failed?

The FAIR framework is a model for building human-centric organizations around the principles I've just described. The four outcomes of FAIR are:

Fairness

Fairness is when all people are set up for success and protected against discrimination.

Given people's differing identities, experiences, and needs, fairness isn't achieved simply by treating everyone in exactly the same way, but by building workplace policies, processes, and practices to prevent bias, maintain accountability, and meet a range of needs while ensuring the same high standard of experience for everyone.

We measure fairness by looking at the major touchpoints of a person's interaction with their environment. In the workplace, that means examining how people's experiences differ regarding pay, promotion, resources, opportunities, discipline, learning, and feedback. If we find major differences in experience—for example, older workers consistently report being paid less than their younger colleagues in the same roles, or candidates without an Ivy League background are consistently passed over for promotion compared to their equally experienced Ivy League–grad colleagues, or neurodivergent workers are pushed into a more limited set of career tracks compared to their neurotypical colleagues—we can investigate potential unfairness and make corrections to policies, processes, or practices to fix the problem.

In one organization I worked with, a senior leader was dealing with a situation where a manager reporting to him had been accused of promoting her team members for personal reasons rather than readiness. Rather than singling out this manager alone for remedial bias training, I worked with the organization to protect against discrimination more broadly by formalizing the promotions process: requiring promotion criteria to be transparent, clarifying these criteria to focus on demonstrated performance rather than assumed potential, standardizing the evaluation process with rubrics, and upskilling decision-makers to utilize this process with confidence.

Improving systems rather than "fixing" individuals requires change management, not a onetime intervention. Luckily, this approach may resonate strongly with what workers already value. Everyone wants a workplace free from favoritism and discrimination, where everyone has the support they need to do their best work and is rewarded fairly for their efforts. Framing FAIR work in these terms can make it clear that a healthier workplace is good for everyone and secure the broad support needed to change the status quo for the better.

Access

Access is when all people can fully participate in a product, service, experience, or physical environment.

While it is closely related to accessibility, access applies to more than disability. Achieving access requires removing barriers to participation and designing products, services, experiences, and environments that work for all. For example, if frontline workers aren't given the means or time to participate in a major virtual celebration that their headquarters colleagues are putting on, the event is inaccessible. If a major all-hands meeting is scheduled on a Jewish or Muslim holiday, the meeting is inaccessible.

To measure access, we look at people's participation and engagement with the various aspects of their environment. We can use metrics like attendance, utilization, or completion rate and collect additional data through tools like the Accessible Usability Scale or user feedback. If we find major differences in experience—for example, workers with children are not attending a monthly networking event because it takes place during typical day care pickup hours—we can investigate potential inaccessibility and correct the product, service, experience, or environment to fix the problem.

Addressing access means organizations should adopt new standard practices in design and development. Too often leaders treat lack of access as an isolated issue to solve on a case-by-case basis and approve sloppy shortcuts that don't solve the root cause of inaccessibility. Imagine a building manager who, instead of installing a ramp to make an entrance accessible, tasks a staff member with manually pushing wheelchair users up the stairs. Because the needs of users outside the norm are not made a standard part of the design or development process, products, services, experiences, and environments end up making the same errors again and again—a phenomenon known as accessibility debt.

To successfully embed user input and feedback into development cycles, practitioners must challenge people's assumptions that prioritizing access is costly and time-consuming—it is far less so than accessibility debt—and demonstrate that doing so is possible. Expanding access for those outside the status quo can result in surprising benefits for everyone, even those who may not think of themselves as having access needs, builds more resilient organizations, and contributes to the independence, dignity, and agency of all people.

Inclusion

Inclusion is when all people feel respected, valued, and safe for who they are.

Inclusion is about engaging thoughtfully with what makes people different, ensuring that given the diversity of people's identities, experiences, beliefs, and perspectives, all can feel respected, valued, and safe. If mostly remote workers feel just as valued by leadership as their mostly in-person counterparts, that's remote/in-person inclusion. If the workplace is a physically safe place to work and a psychologically safe place to share critical feedback, experience productive conflict, or take risks for workers of all genders, that's gender inclusion.

To measure inclusion, we can administer surveys and assessments of people's feelings and experiences within an environment. We can ask about their experiences with physical and psychological safety, their comfort reporting and seeking out support for discrimination if it occurs, and their feelings of respect or disrespect while at work. If we find major differences in experience—for example, LGBTQ+ workers report experiencing physical harassment more frequently than their non-LGBTQ+ colleagues do—we can investigate potential exclusion, offer feedback and accountability to those involved, and correct the environment to fix the problem.

Inclusion is ultimately a matter of workplace norms and culture. Workplaces often address inclusion through event programming (think "lunch and learns" or cultural heritage celebrations), but these shallow attempts at celebration or education rarely change language or behavior ingrained within the status quo. An immigrant experiencing xenophobic threats at work is most supported by a standard protocol that meets their safety needs and addresses threatening behavior at the source—not by asking them to participate in a "cultural diversity celebration." An introverted person who is often spoken over in meetings is most directly supported by meeting agendas sent before each meeting and managers with meeting facilitation skills, not a 50-minute lunch event attended by 10 people on the "power of introverts."

To actually change culture—the set of shared values, expectations, and beliefs for how people engage with each other—leaders and practitioners must do more than share aspirational lists of dos and don'ts tied to specific identity groups. Storytelling, formal authority, and social incentives are all more effective tools for shifting behavior away from unwanted norms and toward desired ones. I once advised a leader who wanted to use their authority to replace a meeting norm of "loudest voice wins" with a five-minute silent period before every discussion for everyone to write down their talking points. This simple practice, communicated clearly and upheld consistently, helped shift the implicit norms among the team. Rewarding and celebrating those who act inclusively, setting expectations for inclusive communication and behavior, and building shared group identity around being respectful and inclusive people are effective strategies for improving inclusion that any leader can utilize.

Representation

Representation is when all people feel their needs are advocated for by those who represent them.

Representation isn't as simple as demographic box-checking. Representation requires participatory decision-making processes, frequent and transparent communications between leaders and key partners, and high trust in leadership from the many different groups they represent built off a track record of accountability. If leaders consistently promise that they will listen to workers experiencing exclusion but then refuse to meet with them, those workers lack representation, even if they technically have a designated representative on the leadership team. If a product team aims to build products for all people but does not consult or include perspectives from a key audience in their design process, that audience lacks representation, even if a member of the product team shares an identity with that audience.

To measure representation, we can collect self-reported data from surveys and assessments on people's feelings about leadership, influence, voice, and trust. We can ask about their trust in leadership, the degree to which they feel like their opinions are solicited and valued, and the degree to which decision-makers consider needs like theirs. If we find major differences in experience—for example, Black workers reporting feeling most unheard and excluded from decisions impacting them compared to other colleagues—we can investigate potential lack of representation and correct communication, behavior, and decision-making processes to fix the problem.

Representation is a matter of trust, not tokenism. While people may be slightly more inclined to trust those who share identities in common with them, trust is more dependent on the behavior and track record of those in power. It's possible for a leadership team made up entirely of women to be nonrepresentative of women if none of the leaders take the effort to understand and advocate for the needs of the women they supposedly represent. On the other hand, it's possible that a product team without direct experience living in rural communities might be very representative of rural communities due to frequent communication, active outreach, and ongoing efforts to understand and advocate for rural communities' needs.

Focusing on representation as an issue of trust rather than an issue of identity allows us to avoid zero-sum conversations that can come from fixating on demographics. Assuming no change in team size, teams populated only with white men must necessarily lose white men if they are to gain women or people of color. This framing instantly activates the common fear that efforts to increase diversity are coming for the jobs and opportunities of white men and other majority group members and lowers the possibility of productive dialogue. If practitioners can instead start a conversation about how much different groups trust and feel heard by leadership, taking seriously those who don't feel represented regardless of their identity or background, we can avoid zero-sum mindsets and the backlash they engender.

Does this mean demographics don't matter? Not at all, but demographic parity (having a workforce demographic mix that mirrors that of customers or society) is an issue of fairness, not representation. So long as leaders are engaged in making work-place systems like hiring, promotion, and feedback more fair, demographic change will be a lagging indicator of progress. In the meantime, today's leaders have actionable goals to strive toward if they want to become more representative of those they serve, regardless of the identities these leaders possess.

. . .

Whether leaders and practitioners choose to adopt the FAIR acronym or not, many of the DEI leaders I spoke to discussed the urgent need for status quo DEI work to evolve.

"'DEI' was great, it had a run. We have to get really good with the fact that things evolve," urged Amber Cabral, founder of leadership development firm Cabral Co. "So let's not be so com-mitted to a group of words and yet be so divorced from how they actually show up in meaningful ways."

"An area missing in DEI work was embracing that the work requires change," said communications strategist Kim Clark. "DEI tended to stay at the top level of organizations, per-haps exemplified as a branded external campaign, rather than empowering every department, every team, and every employee. This led to performative communications that caused more harm than good."

"I see [an] opportunity to go beyond the perfunctory, performative, and symbolic," said Zach Nunn, CEO and founder of Living Corporate, an experience management company. "This is where this space is going; in some ways, the critical season [we are experiencing now] is a good thing."

"FAIR addresses the reality [that] the current workplace has been failing everyone in different ways," said W. Brad Johnson, PhD, a professor at the United States Naval Academy. "For instance, more and more majority men who become fathers want to share more equitably in caregiving, but the calcified workplace may not grant them equitable access to parental leave and flex work. FAIR would level the playing field for men, women, mothers, and fathers in this area."

As your organization continues to navigate anti-DEI backlash, challenge yourself and your leaders to look beyond the DEI status quo. Ensure that as your language, initiatives, and strategies evolve, you are grounding them in outcomes rather than intentions, debiasing systems rather than fixing individuals, creating broad coalitions rather than polarized cliques, and communicating the win-win value of this work rather than giving in to zero-sum narratives. Ensure that whatever you call the work, you are building an organization for tomorrow that is better for everyone in it than it is today.

Adapted from hbr.org, January 23, 2025. Reprint H08LGU

8

For Success with AI, Bring Everyone On Board

by David De Cremer

AI is intimidating your employees. As machines increasingly perform intellectually demanding tasks that were previously reserved for humans, your people feel more excluded and less necessary than ever. And the problem is getting worse. According to the market research company Vanson Bourne, 80% of organizations say that their main technological goal is hyperautomation—the end-to-end automation of as many business processes as possible. Executives have a tendency to pursue that goal without any feedback from their employees—the people whose jobs, and lives, will be most affected by achieving it. But my decades of research into the enterprise adoption of emerging technologies has proved one thing time and again: The savviest leaders prioritize participation by the rank and file throughout the adoption process.

When employees are excluded from that process, they become averse to working with AI, never develop trust in its capabilities, and resist even the positive changes that come from using it. Nonetheless, done correctly, human-AI collaborations represent the most promising way of working. They may not always be the fastest, cheapest, or easiest way to introduce and use artificial intelligence, but the alternative, which excludes workers, is no alternative at all. Consider one example, from researchers at New York University's Center for Cybersecurity. The research team used Copilot, a tool developed by GitHub to generate code automatically, to produce 1,692 software programs with no input from human coders. Forty percent of those programs had critical security flaws.

In this article I examine what keeps leaders from including rank-and-file employees in AI projects, how they should model inclusive behavior, and what your organization must do to develop employee-inclusive AI practices. Those practices can make your long-term performance more likely to improve and your employees more likely to be happy, productive, and engaged.

Becoming Comfortable with AI

You can't bring everyone into the AI adoption process if you're not heavily involved yourself. But business leaders often ask me how they can guide an AI-based transformation when they have no personal expertise with the technology.

Business leaders don't have to be AI experts. They only need to be AI-savvy enough to recognize the technology's benefits for the organization and its stakeholders. Once AI has been deployed, leaders must learn to empower and drive human-AI collaborations. For example, they should be able to identify opportunities for AI integration in everyday workflows and to

Idea in Brief

The Problem

When employees are excluded from the adoption process, they become averse to working with AI, never develop trust in its capabilities, and resist even the positive changes that come from using it.

The Cause

Eighty percent of organizations say their main technological goal is hyperautomation—the end-to-end automation of as many business processes as possible. Executives often pursue that goal without feedback from employees—the people whose jobs and lives will be most affected by achieving it.

The Solution

AI transformation requires constant human-to-human connection across business disciplines. Including rank-and-file employees in AI projects will make your long-term performance more likely to improve—and your employees more likely to be happy, productive, and engaged.

anticipate its potential advantages for teams and projects associated with the technology. In short, learning must be part of their ongoing AI leadership.

Some executives in my advanced leadership classes have wondered aloud whether they need to become professional coders to be effective leaders. What they need is not coding expertise but a foundational understanding of the technology.

The Basics of AI

Most managers know that AI tools are computational systems that have autonomous learning ability. They understand that AI can learn from large datasets and engage in pattern recognition and problem-solving. They've probably already seen it used in a variety of organizational applications: scanning the résumés of job applicants, evaluating employee performance, optimizing task scheduling, managing inventory, and automating repetitive tasks so that employees can explore new ideas and promote innovation rather than count widgets. It's AI's ability to learn—using algorithms to process new data and change its computation of information based on that data—that results in comparisons to human intelligence. But too many business leaders implicitly assume that AI can take over almost any position from humans.

The reality is that AI cannot think like a human, and it isn't all that creative. First, it generates no novel ideas; its ideas exist in the datasets that are fed into it. Not even the most sophisticated AI systems can infer *meaning* from learning, as humans do. They cannot draw analogies, and they cannot appreciate cultural and contextual nuances. Whereas humans can extract the deeper meanings and intricate nuances of business conversations, AI cannot tell when what is said is contradictory to what is meant. For example, it will interpret "You're serious about this offer?" as a simple request to confirm what is being offered. Most humans will understand that the other party is unhappy with what is being offered.

Business leaders who are just AI-savvy enough recognize that the technology can do much to improve work efficiency and the overall functioning of an organization. They must also recognize that it cannot entirely replace humans and, most important, it cannot do our thinking for us.

Three Ways AI Can Alienate Employees

Once you've become comfortable with your ability to discuss and champion AI adoption, you'll need to generate enthusiasm throughout the rank and file—not an easy process. To be an effective leader, you must understand why AI causes a rift between your workers and management and find ways to bridge the gap between what they're feeling about it and what you'd like them to feel. And you'll need to prevent the territorialism and tribalism that can occur when one group controls AI and another doesn't even understand it.

Here are three common reasons for workers' alienation.

Employees lose autonomy and become cynical

Not long ago a colleague of mine applied for a credit card at her bank. The employee helping her entered all her information into a computer program, which ran an algorithm to determine whether she qualified. My colleague, who earns a good living and has good credit, was surprised when the employee informed her that the algorithm had decided she did not qualify for the card. When she asked for an explanation, he replied that the decision was fact-based and automated, so he could not add much to it. Eventually he mumbled that he was not a machine, so why should she expect him to understand the algorithm's decision? That comment revealed that the employee did not feel in control of his job, was clearly demotivated, and had no intention of trying to make the algorithm's decision comprehensible to my colleague. The result was poor customer service and a missed business opportunity.

When you automate easy tasks but leave difficult and emotionally demanding ones to humans, you negatively affect the well-being of your workers. A 2021 study from Georgia State University revealed that the more automation is introduced in the workplace, the worse employee health and job satisfaction become.

Employees don't understand AI and resist it

People generally prefer to work with and receive advice from humans rather than AI. You should be aware of this bias and recognize that employees will respond emotionally rather than rationally to the technology—even when it has proved to be superior to humans.

If you want to make AI adoption inclusive, you must position yourself as both a mediator and a facilitator in human-AI interactions. You need to ensure that your employees receive adequate support and training to interact effectively with AI systems and to create opportunities for them to turn to a human if those interactions go wrong. If they feel truly included in how you plan to work with AI, they will be less averse to it.

A failure to be inclusive may even lead to active resistance. For example, when workers at Amazon's packing facilities were "supervised" by AI algorithms, they became more injury-prone. They were forced to meet high productivity targets, with few if any opportunities to take a break, and could be indiscriminately fired for not hitting their targets. Frustrated, they signed petitions and gathered outside their warehouses, united by the rallying cry *"We are not robots!"* Indeed, as one employee succinctly put it, "[Productivity is] all they care about. They don't care about their employees. They care more about the robots than they care about the employees."

If you want to avoid resistance from your employees when introducing AI, you must push them out of their comfort zone while ensuring that they understand why you're doing so. They should know how you plan to take care of them during this transition. You'll need to exercise patience, because it will take time and effort for workers to become familiar with AI and see how it can help them in their jobs.

AI creates business silos

In addition to eliciting resistance, AI adoption can undermine inclusiveness by entrenching silos in your organization in three ways. First, because the deep expertise required to understand and operate AI systems is often found only in tech teams, employees in other departments (such as HR, operations, and marketing) may have difficulty interacting with AI. But they need the know-how to make use of it in ways that are meaningful to their own business goals. Second, data ownership and access can be a contentious issue between departments. AI systems rely heavily on data for training and decision-making, but individual teams may have their own data repositories and be unwilling or unable to share data with others. Third, the impact AI has will vary across teams: Some may find it more useful than others do, and some may see it being used to automate their tasks more than the tasks in other departments. When different teams feel more or less threat (or benefit) from the adoption of AI, they may turn to siloed behavior, avoiding collaboration and information sharing to protect their own interests.

Employee resistance often creates an organization in which experts in AI and those in business work separately. People mentally shut down and live within the realm of their own expertise. And when AI is adopted differently across silos, resources may be duplicated or underutilized, limiting leaders' ability to scale up the technology across the organization. Teams may collect, store, and manage data independently, resulting in inconsistencies, redundancy, or incomplete datasets. That can hinder your ability to leverage the full potential of your data. When departments operate in isolation, cross-functional collaboration and interdisciplinary problem-solving become impossible. It will be your job as an inclusive leader to stress the importance of collaboration and push for the implementation of technological and organizational solutions, such as centralizing data for analysis in cloud-based tools.

To address all these challenges, you need to adjust your organization's culture.

A More Effective and Inclusive Model for AI

As a business leader, you have to make people feel like full-fledged members of your organization—empowered to work like human beings while collaborating with AI in every automated process. AI can quickly produce code for new programs, for example, but human employees are needed to fix any security flaws and other glitches.

An inclusive approach will make employees feel in control of the adoption process, reduce aversion to the technology, and increase trust in it. Those outcomes will help integrate it more efficiently in your employees' workflow and will enhance the likelihood of creating value across the organization (rather than establishing only siloed, and thus minor, effects). To achieve them, the organization must consistently follow four practices.

Create space and time for social connection

When working with AI, people have to spend a lot of time in front of computer screens communicating with machines. That limits their interaction with other humans. A 2022 poll by the Pew Research Center revealed that a major concern people have about the presence of artificial intelligence in their lives is that it isolates them from other humans. As a leader, you have an important responsibility to foster the social connections of your employees, which you can do through events and online communities within and outside the organization. Digital under-writers, for example, often issue insurance policies without even meeting applicants. They could be asked to have weekly meetings with other underwriters and with the people who built the AI system they use to discuss possible improvements. Uber now allows its drivers, who are under constant algorithmic supervision and feel dehumanized as a result, to telephone other people in the organization when they need help or have a question.

The *Fortune* 500 dairy company Land O'Lakes provides an excellent example of how to free employees from the solitude of working with AI. It began its AI transformation in 2017, when it sought to partially automate commodity forecasting and propensity modeling. Company leaders prioritized speaking with the rank and file about the expected challenges, helping establish a common understanding of the project's possibilities and limits and assuring people that the company wasn't pursuing tech for the sake of tech. Teams coordinated across departments, but company leaders also conducted weekly people-to-people check-ins with every business unit to address any challenges, emotional or procedural, that may have arisen. That approach was crucial to the success of Land O'Lakes' AI transformation. Employees were given opportunities to voice concern, to question tactics, and to raise anything else that might be on their minds.

Make tech and nontech teams collaborate

As an AI-savvy leader, you know that successful human-AI collaborations cross disciplines. Your tech and business experts should not retreat to their separate corners, literal and virtual. So build diverse teams that work together to adopt AI. For example, business experts can explain to tech experts what goals must be achieved, and tech experts can make suggestions regarding which AI systems will be needed. Meanwhile, HR can familiarize employees with the AI system they'll be using and the skills they'll require, and operational staffers can focus on integrating the entire human-AI workflow into the organizational setup.

To lead such diverse teams and bring them together, you must communicate in ways that unite rather than divide people, allowing for and integrating multiple perspectives and identifying roadblocks that may complicate or prevent collaboration. As a business leader, you can start by explaining the organization's needs to your tech and business teams and then outline how the tech experts will become part of the business process to achieve the desired results. Try to establish a common language and understanding for both groups regarding how to approach challenges, recognize patterns, break big problems down into smaller ones, and find a shared work method. Without that common language, your teams may fail to cohere, and the inclusive culture you've tried to develop may dissipate.

In one of my consulting projects I watched the chief technology officer of a global financial institution present the company's new tech strategy. Just a few minutes in, the CEO interrupted. He said he didn't understand anything the CTO was saying and pressured him to present his message in three simple bullet points. It was embarrassing for the CTO. The tech team retrenched. IT departments stopped trying to talk to top executives. The CEO lost credibility with senior executives, who realized he wouldn't be capable of guiding the bank through its AI-adoption project. He hadn't become AI-savvy, didn't connect AI to the purpose of the company, and, worst of all, had not developed the inclusive mindset needed to translate from the

CTO to the business and back. Needless to say, the project failed. The CEO left the company the following year.

When done properly, mixing teams can fundamentally improve not only a company's technology but also its overall culture. In 2017 the agricultural equipment maker CNH Industrial's leadership team decided it wanted to create a host of AI-powered automation capabilities. It also wanted to connect customers with internal and external partners and promote CNH as a service-oriented business.

The executives began the transformation process by speaking with employees from its commercial vehicle unit, industry-specific vehicle units, IT, and operations. Digital advisers and a new digital team were created within CNH's existing IT organization to support ongoing strategy, implementation, and execution. By establishing cross-disciplinary teams and keeping them involved throughout the process, CNH was able to quickly adopt (or retire) experimental approaches. It lowered the barriers between developers and business owners, and it allowed for real-time feedback on scheduled work.

Constantly develop your own leadership skills

Making your employees feel included in your AI adoption project requires that you account for their uncertainty and discomfort when dealing with AI. As an AI-savvy leader, you should be seen as open to listening to their concerns. My research indicates that employees are indeed more willing to trust and engage with AI if their leaders are humble and demonstrate that openness.

Consider Satya Nadella, the CEO of Microsoft, who is a master at using empathy to foster inclusion. One of the first things he did when he was appointed CEO, in 2014, was to persuade his employees that no matter how successful Microsoft had been in the past, they should stay open to new ideas and other ways of working. Asking them to think differently required courage, but it also showed the importance of being humble—unafraid of receiving feedback from others. A humble attitude in a leader encourages employees to interact regularly with experts in different departments to understand and relate to the diverse perspectives at work in the organization.

You must also guide employees in their understanding of AI. For human-AI interactions to be truly collaborative, employees need strong frameworks for thinking about how to work with smart machines. In airline safety, for example, pilots need more training to fly planes with collaborative autopilot systems. That's because, as Captain Shem Malmquist, a veteran safety and aviation accident investigator, told *Wired* in 2022, they "must have a mental model of both the aircraft and its primary systems, as well as how the flight automation works" to manage issues that could turn into catastrophic crashes. Only when employees have a clear model of their own strengths and weaknesses, and those of their AI tools, will they understand how AI can augment their work.

Reward workers for being human

Employees want you to tell them how you see their role in the human-AI collaborative process. They also want to know how they will be rewarded for the value that collaboration creates. For humans and AI to work together successfully, you need to establish clear guidelines for who is credited with what. Otherwise your employees may feel that you've downplayed their contribution and attributed the project's success largely to the AI.

To ensure that employees feel included, let them share in the rewards that come with the value that AI creates. Emphasize that in your view, humans are crucial to the performance of AI and therefore deserve appropriate acknowledgment. Even just a companywide email recognizing and celebrating someone's accomplishments can go a long way toward boosting morale.

. . .

AI adoption is a complex process that requires everyone involved to learn, question, and collaborate. How your company approaches it will depend on the level of your employees' technological acumen, your budget, and many other critical factors. But the approach I recommend is one that any company can take to optimize the process.

It should begin with managers' learning just enough about AI to feel confident communicating its importance to their teams. Then you need constant human-to-human connection among cross-disciplinary business units as well as meetings at which everyone feels free to speak openly. Such gatherings provide excellent opportunities for managers to show vulnerability, communicate their own questions, or even just listen to venting among colleagues. When your transformation is underway, and your business is focused on optimizing AI rather than simply implementing it, you should reward your employees for their uniquely human contributions. If they don't feel valued and respected, your transformation attempt will certainly fail.

Originally published in May–June 2024. Reprint R2403J

9

Design Products That Won't Become Obsolete

by Vijay Govindarajan, Tojin T. Eapen, and Daniel J. Finkenstadt

In 2017 Radio Flyer, the maker of the iconic Little Red Wagon, introduced a remote-controlled, battery-operated car that kids can ride on. It has three modes of operation, each of which is suited to a different growth stage for young children. In stage one the car is controlled remotely by a watchful parent. In stage two the child drives the car, but parents can override any questionable decisions. In stage three all driving decisions, safe or concerning, are made by the child. Radio Flyer gave its new product a simple name, one that made its abilities and selling points perfectly clear: the Grow with Me Racer.

The Grow with Me Racer is just one of many commercial offerings today that can change and expand to suit users' evolving needs. We, an academic and two consultants with more than 20 years' worth of experience studying product development, refer to them as "products that grow." In recent years they've become more numerous and ever more complex. Consider the Google Android and Apple iOS operating systems, which are routinely updated to add capabilities to smartphones. Tesla improves the performance of its cars nearly every month by issuing software upgrades. John Deere can add features to its harvesting combine machines through software upgrades, without altering the hardware. Senior citizens can now overcome the creeping impairment of presbyopia with tunable eyeglass lenses made by Deep Optics. Medical researchers are testing implantable pediatric devices, including a heart valve and stent, that can grow with the bodies of their young recipients. Even the content of this article is a product that grows. Through an online GPT, accessible at ptgchat.com, users can apply the article's principles to various contexts and access advice that is regularly updated with new information.

Such products offer enormous potential to companies and their customers. Their ability to evolve can greatly extend their useful life, eliminating or postponing the need for replacements and allowing users to become more familiar with them, two factors that increase *customer value*. Delaying or removing the need to manufacture replacements promotes *sustainability*, conserving energy, reducing harmful emissions, and slowing the accumulation of toxic materials. Products that grow offer a way out of the ecological quicksand of planned obsolescence, a profitable but wasteful strategy that consumers dislike. They help companies protect their reputations and save consumers money.

Building a product that grows isn't always as easy as updating software, however. Knowing what consumers want today can be difficult; now companies will have to predict what customers will want five or 10 years from now. That will require firms to rethink how they develop and design new products. And because

Idea in Brief

The Opportunity

Products that grow, or adaptable products, offer more value than products that aren't designed to change.

The Challenge

Knowing what consumers want today can be difficult. To create adaptable products, companies will have to predict what customers will want five or 10 years from now.

The Payoff

Brands that can build adaptable products will be seen as pioneers in a market that increasingly emphasizes flexibility, longevity, and environmental consciousness.

adaptable products may be harder to build or repair than traditional ones, companies will need to figure out how to avoid driving up the total cost of ownership. Continual software updates also may make users worry about losing control over their personal data or becoming more vulnerable to security breaches. Finally, users may find themselves burdened with features or functionality that exceed their wants and needs.

Despite those concerns, we believe that products that grow will serve businesses well. Managers who switch to them from static products will position their organizations for success in a market that increasingly emphasizes adaptability, longevity, and environmental consciousness. The era of use-and-throw-away will be replaced by a new age of use-and-grow, allowing companies to harmonize customer needs and sustainability demands. In this article we'll examine the categories of offerings that are already benefiting from this approach, and we'll detail how companies can begin to integrate products that grow into their current strategies.

Ways That Products Can Grow

Adaptable products aren't a new phenomenon. But modern technology has made it easier to create them. Thirty years ago software was released in a single, final version, but today digital products, like your phone's operating system or apps, can be immediately adjusted and improved through software updates. Hardware products, like smart appliances, can be equipped with software that changes their functionality in real time. Any company with digital offerings can use software to upgrade products and lengthen their lives.

Products that grow are already revolutionizing education, toys, sports equipment, and other markets. Toys and games that teach coding to children, for instance, are designed to unlock new features or challenges as kids reach new skill levels. One of them, Learning Resources' game Switcheroo Coding Crew, features modifiable vehicles and a 46-piece interactive play set. Moxie, a teaching robot for autistic children aged five to 10, tailors its lessons to the knowledge of its users. Training equipment for sports teams and productivity tools for work teams can both track the joint progress of multiple users and adapt their functions to suit the group's skill level.

Our study of the market for adaptable products, which looked at more than 150 products from a wide variety of industries, reveals that they've been helping customers overcome seven challenges, including some they've been addressing for decades:

1. *Age-related developments.* As children grow, they often need products that can be modified to suit their increased size and skills.

2. *Age-related challenges.* At the other end of the spectrum, the abilities of older users (such as vision or physical

strength) often decline in ways that gradually alter the products they need.

3. *Congenital limitations.* Medical conditions and physical disabilities can evolve over the course of people's lifetimes and generate new requirements for support.

4. *Desire for novelty.* Customers often lose interest in products that stay the same.

5. *Shifting learning needs.* The difficulty and volume of information presented to students need to be set at the level that's currently appropriate for them.

6. *Technological evolution.* Changes to features and underlying technical specifications often prompt a need for upgrades.

7. *Shifting performance needs.* Many kinds of machinery and equipment require constant mechanical improvements.

How Adaptable Products Are Built

Companies can meet those challenges in four distinct ways. The approach that works best for your company will depend on your industry expertise, the new product, and your technical acumen.

Configurable hardware

Some products have hardware that can be adjusted to users' needs. They include wheelchairs with modular bases that can grow, shrink, or be reformatted as the customers' medical equipment and storage needs evolve. Another example is Radio Flyer's 4-in-1 Stroll 'N Trike, which can morph from an infant tricycle, to a steering tricycle, to a learning-to-ride tricycle, to a classic tricycle to suit riders of varying abilities.

Preconfigured software

Some products learn from and adapt to the user to improve her experience as her knowledge of them evolves. Smart sports equipment, for example, contains software that gives athletes feedback on how to improve their performance.

Updatable hardware

These products are designed for customization and repair. Take smart security systems, which offer modules that allow users to add new physical devices, such as fingerprint scanners, facial recognition cameras, and advanced motion sensors.

Updatable software

Unlike preconfigured software, some software receives constant updates that enhance products over time. The user may request an update, or the manufacturer may push it out. Smart cars that get software updates and smart thermostats whose algorithms are tweaked to increase heating and cooling efficiency are both examples.

A Competitive Advantage

Across these categories of products, there are several ways companies can separate themselves from the competition.

Increased engagement

A product that grows allows a company to forge valuable longer-term connections with customers. With both digital and analog products, the company can involve customers throughout the product life cycle, bringing them into the product development process and regularly probing them for insights into new opportunities rather than just gathering their feedback on existing products. Such interactions build more-enduring relationships, strengthening brand loyalty and value. Eventually they can even foster the growth of communities around a product, which take on the task of identifying ways to improve it. OpenAI's launch of custom GPTs is a good example. The company allows customers who pay for a premium ChatGPT subscription to tailor the baseline GPT-4o model to specific use cases. The user can also offer the resulting custom models for sale on the firm's GPT store, a capability that drives engagement through monetary rewards and the intrinsic motivators of creativity, autonomy, mastery, and social connection.

Flexible market response

Products that grow allow companies to react quickly to changing market demands and evolving consumer preferences. The strategic integration of adaptable features can also help companies attract new customers without undertaking a product overhaul.

Consider the electronics startup Fairphone, which prioritizes sustainability and ethical production. Its smartphones have a modular design that lets users easily replace or upgrade key components like the battery, screen, and camera without professional assistance. That not only extends the device's lifespan but enables the company to adapt to market trends by offering new features.

Continual innovation

Unlike products with static designs, products that grow may require regular improvement even after they reach the hands of customers. This forces companies to perpetually innovate, which can help push them to the forefront of the market.

Positive social impact

The longer life of products that grow shrinks their environmental footprint. As we've noted, companies generate less waste and use fewer resources when there's less need to dispose of products and manufacture and market replacements for them. The cost of disposal can be very high in many countries, so products that grow can significantly reduce the amount of money spent on managing refuse. While the relative complexity of some adaptable products might make them more difficult or costly to dispose of, they still minimize the product returns that pile up in landfills. In an era when businesses are evaluated for their environmental and social impact, products that grow can help their makers position themselves as responsible organizations with a strong social purpose.

Models for Capturing Value

Some companies may worry, understandably, that adaptable products may be less profitable in the long run than traditional products are. After all, companies that sell more products make more money, and planned obsolescence has been the quiet engine driving much of 20th-century commerce. But there's plenty of evidence that the products-that-grow approach can be profitable, whether adopted as an overarching business strategy or as a component of a broader company program that strives to balance customer focus and sustainability. Software-enhanced vehicles that allow users to update features on demand are expected to create $650 billion in value for the auto industry by the end of the decade, for example. Fairphone increased annual sales of its modular products from 88,000 units in 2021 to 170,000 in

2023 and was profitable for three straight years from 2020 to 2022. (In 2023 it decided to make a big investment in its future growth and took a loss.) With the help of its adaptable products, Radio Flyer's revenues and profit grew at a compounded rate of 10% annually from 2018 to 2023.

Several pricing and business models for adaptable products can help companies grow the value pie and share it with their customers.

Premium pricing

Because an adaptable product can replace multiple purchases of similar products, a company can charge more for it. In the footwear industry, Because International, a nonprofit that fights poverty, has created the Shoe That Grows, an affordable shoe that expands five sizes and lasts for years. If a for-profit company sold an expandable kids' shoe, it could price the shoe higher than a single-size one but below the total paid for additional pairs of larger sizes. Though the company would earn more profit per unit, the customers' overall costs would fall.

Charging for upgrades

Makers of some products, such as smartphones, could offer a subscription service that regularly adds new features like premium content or exclusive functionality. Companies could also charge extra for personalization and product modifications.

Products as services

Companies can sell adaptable products as services. A business can retain ownership of them and simply charge its customers for every use. The Moxie robot, for instance, has a subscription model: The pricey learning tool can be rented for $100 a month.

Complementary products

The prolonged life cycle of products that grow gives companies greater opportunities to develop complementary products. Along with accessories like headphones, earbuds, chargers, and protective cases, Fairphone sells replacement parts for its products and a custom screwdriver for installing them.

Complementary services

Manufacturers can charge for services such as monitoring (for medical products) or training programs (for sports equipment) associated with a product's use.

Monetizing maintenance

Because adaptable products last longer than most offerings, they may need more repairs. Companies can make money by selling their users product warranties and extended guarantees. While industrial and B2B products that need complex repairs traditionally profit from this model, consumer goods companies are now adopting similar strategies. Keurig, for instance, has done so in the coffee industry.

Keurig's K-Duo line of coffee makers, which are capable of brewing both a single cup and a full carafe, caters to diverse consumer needs. At the same time, K-Duo has streamlined manufacturing processes: Making an all-in-one product is simpler and more efficient than making multiple kinds of coffee makers. By offering maintenance kits for these machines, Keurig has opened new revenue streams and supported right-to-repair initiatives. The coffee makers' extended life cycle also reduces Keurig's competition risks. This is a great example of how a company can simultaneously lower its production costs and generate recurring revenue through maintenance solutions, creating a win-win scenario for both the business and its customers.

Brand communities

Adaptable products offer an opportunity to establish online platforms or forums where users can exchange experiences, tips, and customization ideas related to the product. Companies can introduce a membership fee for access to premium features, exclusive content, or priority customer support within the community. Peloton is a great example of a firm that has done this well.

Resale and modification services

Some products will have multiple owners throughout their life cycle. In such cases a company can offer services for refurbishing or modifying the look or style of a product for reuse and create platforms for resale. This can be done with toys, cars, and industrial equipment. For example, a bike purchased for a child whose interests are in space-themed activities could be modified for use by another child who has an interest in dolls.

These are just a few of the ways companies are monetizing and building competitive advantage with products that grow. As companies experiment with and produce more adaptable products, new models will emerge that provide as much or even more value.

. . .

Integrating products that grow into a business strategy requires a solid commitment to sustainability, customer satisfaction, and perpetual innovation—three things that in the long run will serve companies well. Brands that can make this switch will be seen as pioneers in a market that increasingly rewards adaptability, long-term value, and environmental sustainability.

We predict that technological progress and the increasing complexity of our lives will drive up sales for products that grow. These offerings appeal to young and old alike. They allow companies to meet the changing preferences of consumers and the unending demands of a world that requires faster computers, safer vehicles, and greater efficiency. As the world changes, so must the products we design and sell.

Originally published in November–December 2024. Reprint R2406F

10

The Strategic Genius of Taylor Swift

by Kevin Evers

L ess than two decades since making her debut recording, Taylor Swift has conquered the music industry. She has released 11 original studio albums, and the combined sales and streams of her music catalog place her among the top 10 best-selling artists of all time—a group dominated by commercial juggernauts such as Michael Jackson, Elvis, Madonna, and Frank Sinatra. Her recently concluded Eras Tour—the highest-grossing tour of all time—set off a global frenzy that sparked comparisons to the Beatles. With a net worth estimated at $1.6 billion, Swift is the most financially successful musician of her generation. And she's managed to achieve all this during a time when the industry has undergone profound technological and business model shifts, moving from CDs to iTunes to Spotify.

Historically, musicians have found it difficult to sustain success. Many struggle to maintain relevance or popularity beyond just one or two albums. And the rare artists who do endure typically transition into nostalgia acts. At 35, Swift is already a multigenerational phenomenon: The teenage girls who bought her 2006 debut album are now bringing their own children to her shows. Indeed, Swift's ability to reinvent herself and attract new fans while retaining the core of what her existing fans love is key to her unique cultural momentum.

For more than two years, while writing a book that explores the entire arc of Swift's career, I dived deep into her decision-making, trying to understand how and why she keeps winning. To be sure, Swift positions herself first and foremost as an artist, and she sometimes downplays her role as a strategist. "I never a single time woke up in the morning and thought, 'You know what I'm going to do today? I'm gonna go innovate some stuff,'" Swift said while accepting the Innovator Award at the 2023 iHeartRadio Music Awards. "What I did do was try to make the right decision for me." But despite her protestations, over the years Swift has displayed such a remarkable ability to innovate—and to make sophisticated strategy and marketing moves—that it's worth trying to draw lessons from her career, the same way we study traditional business visionaries such as Steve Jobs, Richard Branson, and Jeff Bezos.

So what is the secret to Swift's long-term success? In my view it can be attributed to four behaviors: targeting untapped markets, finding opportunities to create stickiness, maintaining productive paranoia, and adapting to radical shifts in platforms.

Targeting Untapped Markets

Swift started out with advantages. Born into a Pennsylvania family with show-business ties—her maternal grandmother, Marjorie, was an opera singer—Swift benefited from her parents'

Idea in Brief

The Idea

Even people who don't follow music closely recognize that Taylor Swift has become a global cultural force. What most people don't understand is how much of her success is driven by strategic decision-making.

The Context

When Swift began writing songs, country music was dominated by men and most music was consumed via radio or CD. She's succeeded in an industry undergoing profound technological and business model shifts. That has required her to undergo several phases of reinvention.

The Insight

Swift's success can be attributed to four behaviors: targeting untapped markets, finding opportunities to create stickiness, maintaining productive paranoia, and adapting to radical shifts in platforms. By studying her career, business leaders can draw valuable lessons on innovation and strategic thinking.

unwavering support. They connected her with Britney Spears's former manager, who helped Swift secure a development deal with RCA Records at age 13. And in 2003 her parents moved the entire family near Nashville so that Swift could collaborate with top-notch writers and producers.

In the early 2000s the country music scene operated on principles that had been in place for decades. Few performers wrote their own music; most relied on professional songwriters. And after seeing a wave of successful female artists (including Faith Hill, Shania Twain, and The Chicks) in the 1990s, the genre had shifted back to favoring male performers. Additionally, country radio, which was increasingly controlled by a few large companies, prioritized data-driven playlists, leaving little room for new or unconventional voices.

Instead of focusing on those obstacles, Swift recognized a "blue ocean"—what the strategy gurus W. Chan Kim and Renée Mauborgne call a completely untapped market (in contrast with a bloody "red ocean," where competitors fight over the same customers). "All the songs I heard on the radio were about marriage and kids and settling down. I just couldn't relate to that," Swift told the *Telegraph*. "I felt there was no reason why country music shouldn't relate to someone my age if someone my age was writing it." When her record company encouraged her to collaborate with established songwriters (mostly middle-aged men), Swift would show up with dozens of remarkably fleshed-out songs about middle school crushes and preoccupations, determined to find a way to appeal to listeners in her own demographic.

Her vision drew skepticism. "[People said,] 'Teenagers don't listen to country music. That's not the audience. The audience is a 35-year-old housewife . . . How are you going to relate to those women when you're 16 years old?'" she later told NPR. "And I kept thinking, 'But I love country music, and I'm a teenager!' There have to be more kids out there like me." As her career began taking off after the release of her first album, it became clear: There were.

Swift's intent to target a completely new demographic has parallels to the strategy Marvel used to dominate the comic book industry. Prior to Marvel's creative transformation in the 1960s, DC Comics led the industry by churning out mythical stories for children and teens. To set Marvel apart—and avoid the ruthless competition of a red ocean—editor-in-chief Stan Lee and writer-artists Jack Kirby and Steve Ditko began developing content with more-human and flawed superheroes—the Fantastic Four, the Hulk, Iron Man, the Black Panther—that they marketed to college students and adults, an audience the industry had ignored.

Because it aimed its new product at noncustomers, Marvel had no competition—and in her early years, neither did Swift.

Finding Opportunities to Create Stickiness

When Swift came on the scene, in 2006, the relationship between artists and fans was undergoing significant changes. The internet was making music cheaper and easier to discover, and as social media gave fans greater access and connection, they began to expect more than just a passive listening experience. "The customers' problem is how to navigate and 'do things' with the music they have access to," wrote Queensland University of Technology professor Patrik Wikström in an article about how digital distribution had impacted the music industry. In other words, customer value was becoming less about getting music into fans' hands and more about giving people new ways to engage with it. Swift did that by sharing highly personal and authentic accounts of her own experiences with her young fan base in her lyrics.

Fans' obsession with the words of songs isn't a new phenomenon. A Bob Dylan fan named Alan J. Weberman, a self-proclaimed "Dylanologist," used to transcribe all the songwriter's lyrics on punch cards and alphabetize them in the hopes of uncovering the hidden messages in Dylan's "secret language of rock." Fans scrutinized the covers of Beatles albums (and played the records backward) looking for evidence of Paul McCartney's death. And for decades, people have speculated about the identity of Carly Simon's self-absorbed lover in "You're So Vain." In each of these cases the community's investment was strong. But with Swift there was the internet, which, as it has done to most things, scaled this kind of community engagement up to extreme new levels.

Even people who haven't followed her career or music closely are probably aware that Swift, like many songwriters, has written a fair share of breakup songs. Swift's first ever single, "Tim McGraw," was about a boyfriend who'd gone off to college. Her most recent album, *The Tortured Poets Department*, is thought to be an excavation of her relationship with British rocker Matty Healy of the band The 1975. One of the best early examples, however, is "Dear John" from her 2010 album *Speak Now*—an emotional ballad widely interpreted as a reflection on her rumored relationship with the musician John Mayer. The song is a raw and introspective look at a failed romance. As Swift recalled, it's "sort of like the last email you would ever send to someone that you used to be in a relationship with."

The lyrics on tracks like these are designed to create intrigue for her audience. They provide enough detail to make it seem as if they could be about a person or a situation the listener knows about from the tabloid news or paparazzi photos—but not so much that they're explicitly or definitively so. There's plausible deniability there. By dropping hints, Swift indulges inquisitive fans who like to analyze her songs the way T. S. Eliot scholars dissect *The Waste Land*. The clever clues and the double meanings are discussed and debated endlessly online, and the devoted Swift community grows—and grows closer.

Swift is just taking control of what other artists let happen organically. She understands the assignment: In the social media era, her personal life is a source of constant speculation—especially because it is the inspiration for her songs. Fan theories spread like wildfire whether she wants them to or not, so she might as well play along. She is simply embracing the new rules of the game.

Passionate fan engagement, particularly among young women, has often been dismissed as frivolous or hysterical. Consider the screaming Beatles audiences of the 1960s and the ardent follow-ers of boy bands in the 1990s and 2000s. But by embedding intri-cate clues, references to her personal life, and Easter eggs in her work, Swift validates and rewards her fans' devotion. She treats it as valuable, not vapid.

The more she encourages her fans to interpret her music, the more sophisticated their interpretations become. They analyze complex metaphors, track motifs across albums, and spin the-ories about her artistic vision. And they keep coming back for more. Swift demonstrates that taking fangirl behavior seriously is good business. And now other artists are looking to copy her model.

Maintaining Productive Paranoia

Swift's last 10 original studio albums have reached number one on the Billboard 200—an unprecedented run. But Swift has rarely shown signs of complacency. In fact, she has expressed a constant fear that her success will eventually come to an end. "You can't keep winning and have people like it," she once told *Rolling Stone*. "People love 'new' so much—they raise you up the flagpole, and you're waving at the top of the flagpole for a while. And then they're like, 'Wait, this *new* flag is what we actually love.'"

Swift's self-professed anxiety aligns with a core principle of strategy. As Intel's legendary founder, Andy Grove, famously stated, "Success breeds complacency. Complacency breeds fail-ure. Only the paranoid survive." The leadership experts Jim Collins and Morten Hansen have argued that such worried watchfulness is an essential characteristic of leadership. In a study of leaders who navigated uncertainties and upheavals, from oil crises to technological shifts, they found that one of the things that set successful leaders apart was being highly alert to potential negative developments—a trait they call "productive paranoia."

Looking through a strategy lens, it's apparent that at critical moments, Swift has channeled her fear into creative pivots. Often she has executed them when external signs—album sales, critical response, and award recognition—suggested that doing more of the same was optimal. Frequently she changed direction by carefully choosing a small group of collaborators to help her explore new sounds and genres.

Consider her album *Red*. At the time it was released, in 2012, Swift had become part of a clique—along with Coldplay, Rihanna, Beyoncé, and Adele—that owned a disproportionate share of sales and fans in music. She'd joined this elite group by being an anti-pop-star, in a sense: Drawing on her country roots, her songs were introspective, soft-toned, and often acoustic, countering the pop trend toward anthemic choruses and high-voltage production. But in the middle of writing and recording *Red*, Swift decided to make a major change by collaborating with the Swedish pop producer Max Martin, who is known for crafting massive hits for 'N Sync, the Backstreet Boys, Britney Spears, Kelly Clarkson, Avril Lavigne, and Katy Perry. At the time Martin had a reputation as an auteur-style producer—one who wrote most of the melodies, many of the lyrics, and all the arrangements for his artists. He was the creative force; the artists were the hired guns.

The risk of running toward this approach was in the optics. Swift had positioned herself as a self-made artist, putting her songwriting in the center of her vision and origin story. Her fans valued her more solitary approach to writing and creating music, and she publicly talked up her process and posted behind-the-scenes clips of her writing and studio work. A Swift-Martin partnership would fly in the face of her brand. It could look as if she was chasing hits and had become calculated and inauthentic.

She wound up working with Martin on three of *Red*'s tracks, including "We Are Never Ever Getting Back Together," which became its first single. It's clearly a Swift song, with a verse full of grievances that transforms into a shout-it-from-the-rooftop chorus: "We. Are never, ever, ever. Getting back together." It's also clearly a Martin track: The music slaps, its twisted electric riffs morphing into something fuller with a bed of synth chords, pronounced bass, and several layers of Swift's voice harmonizing. Throw in a minimalist chorus reprise that leads into an I'm-so-over-him spoken-word bridge, and you have Swift's first full foray into pop music.

Critics and fans gave the song mixed reviews. Since Swift's persona was largely based on down-to-earth, hardworking, singer-songwriter traits, some were sure to think that the single disrupted what researchers call her *doxa*—the unwritten norms and behaviors that draw fans to an artist. But in the end the positive shock of bringing in Martin worked. Whatever angst had greeted the single, it didn't create a full-fledged backlash, and the song seemed to grow her audience. It became her first number one Billboard Hot 100 hit, selling 623,000 digital copies in its first week and setting a record for a female artist. The album also topped the charts in the United Kingdom, Canada, and Australia, expanding Swift's reach beyond the United States.

Ever since, Swift has gained a reputation as a shape-shifter. After fully embracing synth pop on a spate of post-*Red* albums—again, with an assist from Martin and a handful of other producers—she teamed up with The National's Aaron Dessner and her frequent collaborator Jack Antonoff of Bleachers in her switch to an indie rock sound on 2020's *Folklore*, her most critically acclaimed album. Her genre-hopping has not only kept her fans engaged but also contributed to her lasting success. Her skillful execution of this strategy has shifted fans' expectations: Her transformations aren't just tolerated; they're eagerly anticipated.

Adapting to Radical Shifts in Platforms

If Swift's rise to superstardom was made possible by her skillful navigation of the digital age, her recent mastery of streaming has elevated her success and popularity.

In truth, she took a while to come around to streaming. Swift is considered a "class 1 superstar," a term that the music-research firm Midia uses to describe artists whose careers started before the streaming era. This status made Swift somewhat immune to the challenges that streaming posed. Her albums received blockbuster-like attention and fanfare, so she didn't need to come up with new, innovative ways to keep people's attention. Because her tours are so profitable, she didn't have to rely on streaming's difficult economics. (Artists generally receive about $0.001 to $0.008 each time a song is played on a streaming service.) And despite music audiences' mass migration onto streaming platforms, Swift continues to sell millions of physical units of CDs and vinyl records. In fact, in 2014 her position was so strong that after a public spat with Spotify's cofounder Daniel Ek about his platform's royalty rates, she pulled her entire catalog from streaming services. (She relented in 2017.) Most artists couldn't afford to do that.

But as streaming took hold, her strategy evolved. From 2015 to 2019, Spotify's paid-subscriber base increased from 15 million to 124 million users—a growth rate of 726%. Streaming has changed content strategies: Before its rise, fans were accustomed to artists' releasing a full-length album every few years. In a streaming-dominant world, the volume of material musicians produce matters because putting out more songs allows them to game the algorithm. The more tracks you release, the more likely one is to break through, and when one does, the algorithm rewards you with more appearances in recommendations, which lead to more clicks. Streams beget streams.

Consider the Canadian rapper Drake, Swift's labelmate at Republic Records. Midia consultant Kriss Thakrar crunched the numbers and found that Drake released 200 new tracks from 2015 to 2023—an average of one new song every 16 days over eight years. Swift, on the other hand, released about 50 tracks in the six-year period from 2014 to 2019. In other words, Swift was precious while Drake was prolific.

Swift's realization that she needed to change strategies coincided with the Covid-19 pandemic. She responded by turning on the fire hose. For much of her career she had released an album every two years. During the pandemic she put out her eighth album, *Folklore*, just 11 months after her seventh album, *Lover*—and then her ninth, *Evermore*, followed less than five months later. In just 15 months she released 52 album tracks—about one song every week and a half.

Then she began rerecording older songs. After her former label head sold her back catalog, Swift remade four of her first six albums (labeling each one "Taylor's Version") to gain more control over her music (and more revenue when fans streamed newer versions of her songs). The albums added new tracks and some longer versions, as well—most notably, "All Too Well (10 Minute Version) (Taylor's Version)." With so many rerecordings flooding the streaming services, Swift effectively broke down the barriers between "new work" and "old work."

It's difficult to overstate how effective this has been. "This is the part about Taylor Swift's career that is unprecedented," wrote *Uproxx*'s Steven Hyden in 2023. "She has, rather brilliantly, convinced the public that her past *and* present coexist *right now* . . ." There are plenty of older artists—Paul McCartney, Bruce Springsteen, Billy Joel—who can fill a stadium and play a greatest-hits set consisting mostly of songs recorded before 1985. In contrast, Swift's streaming strategy and rerecordings have created a sort of time machine that makes fans as excited about her 2024 releases as they are about her 2012 hits. "She gets to be a 'legacy act' and a 'relevant pop act' simultaneously," Hyden wrote. The Eras Tour, which featured minisets devoted to 10 of Swift's original albums (all except her self-titled debut), was the culmination of this achievement.

. . .

At a time of rapid technological change, Swift has positioned herself as an artist who refuses to be confined. Her continued success is more than just a result of her talent—it's a master class in navigating a fast-changing industry with foresight, creativity, and strategic brilliance.

Originally published in March–April 2025. Reprint R2502H

Discussion Guide

Are you feeling inspired by what you've read in this collection? Do you want to share the ideas in the articles or explore the insights you've gleaned with others? This discussion guide offers an opportunity to dig a little deeper, with questions to prompt personal reflection and to start conversations with your team.

You don't need to have read the book from beginning to end to use this guide. Choose the questions that apply to the articles you have read or that you feel might spark the liveliest discussion.

Reflect on key takeaways from your reading to help you adopt the ideas and techniques you want to integrate into your work as a leader. What tools can you share with your team to help everyone be their best? Becoming the leader you want to be starts with a detailed plan—and a commitment to carrying it out.

1. Describe a time when asking questions led to a breakthrough in your team or organization. What made questioning particularly effective? As a leader, how can you balance asking questions while providing direction to your people?

2. Reflect on a project in your organization that you thought was the first of its kind. How did this perception influence your approach to project management? What other projects or industries could you have investigated for similarities? What are some strategies you can use to overcome the pitfalls of uniqueness bias in the future?

3. In multibusiness companies, leaders often focus too much on the makeup of their portfolios, rather than how to manage them. Thinking back to the article by Bharat N. Anand and David J. Collis, what common pitfalls in managing multibusiness strategies apply to your organization? What steps have you taken—or plan to take in the future—to avoid them?

4. How did the results of the A/B test at Trip.com confirm or challenge your views on hybrid work? How did its findings compare with experiences in your own company? Where could you implement your own A/B tests to assess and refine policies in areas beyond hybrid work?

5. Erin Meyer's article, "Build a Corporate Culture That Works," emphasizes grounding your culture in real-world dilemmas. Share an example of a situation where your own organization's values were challenged. How did it influence your corporate culture? How can the concept of "dilemma-testing" help ensure that your organization's values are practical and actionable?

6. According to the article "Why Leadership Teams Fail," there are three main patterns of dysfunction in leadership teams: the shark tank, the petting zoo, and the mediocracy. How have you seen these manifest in your own organization, either as a senior leader yourself or as an observer? What impact did these tensions have? What actions can leaders take to foster a healthier team dynamic?

7. Discuss ways that leaders can foster a culture of rational optimism while remaining realistic about macroeconomic risks. How can your organization improve its approach

to economic forecasting? In what ways can you remain informed, while also avoiding the influence of overly pessimistic predictions?

8. Describe a time when you've asked your manager to advocate for you. In what ways was it successful, and where did your efforts fall short? What would you change, either in the request itself or in the lead-up to your ask, if you made this request again?

9. Lily Zheng's article on what's next for DEI introduces the FAIR framework (fairness, access, inclusion, and representation). What are the benefits or challenges to this model? How should organizations ensure that their policies are perceived as fair by all employees? As a people leader, what can you do to build a healthier workplace with these four outcomes in mind?

10. What is your current experience with encouraging others to use generative AI? How can you address their fears about automation and AI and foster a culture of openness and learning around new technologies? What practices can your organization adopt to ensure AI projects are inclusive and beneficial for all?

11. Reflect on the example of Radio Flyer's Grow with Me Racer. How does this product illustrate the idea of creating products that grow? What opportunities like this exist in your company or industry?

12. Kevin Evers highlights many ways Taylor Swift has used business practices to navigate her successful career in music. What stood out to you about how she incorporated

strategic thinking into her career? How can you apply similar thinking and actions to your own work?

13. What other topics are on your mind that were not covered in this book? What do you see as challenges or opportunities moving forward? What trends did you see in the past year that will shape how you lead in 2026?

About the Contributors

Bharat N. Anand is the Henry R. Byers Professor of Business Administration at Harvard Business School and the vice provost for Advances in Learning at Harvard University.

Jean-Louis Barsoux is a term research professor at IMD and a coauthor of *ALIEN Thinking: The Unconventional Path to Breakthrough Ideas*.

Nicholas Bloom is a professor of economics at Stanford University.

Alexander Budzier is a fellow in management practice in information systems at Saïd Business School.

Philipp Carlsson-Szlezak is a managing director and partner in Boston Consulting Group's New York office and the firm's global chief economist. He is a coauthor of *Shocks, Crises, and False Alarms: How to Assess True Macroeconomic Risk* (Harvard Business Review Press, 2024).

Arnaud Chevallier is a professor of strategy at IMD Business School.

M.D. Christodoulou is a senior statistician in the department of statistics at the University of Oxford.

David J. Collis is an adjunct professor of business administration at Harvard Business School and the winner of the McKinsey Award for the best *Harvard Business Review* article of 2008.

Frédéric Dalsace is a professor of marketing and strategy at IMD.

David De Cremer is a professor of management and technology at Northeastern University and the Dunton Family Dean of its D'Amore-McKim School of Business. He is the author of *The AI-Savvy Leader* (Harvard Business Review Press, 2024). His website is daviddecremer.com.

Tojin T. Eapen is the founder of the Center for Creative Foresight, a senior fellow at the Conference Board, and an adviser at StratRocket.

Kevin Evers is a senior editor at *Harvard Business Review* and the author of *There's Nothing Like This: The Strategic Genius of Taylor Swift* (Harvard Business Review Press, 2025).

Daniel J. Finkenstadt is a U.S. military officer, an academic researcher, and the principal of Wolf Stake Consulting. He is a coauthor of the books *Supply Chain Immunity* and *Bioinspired Strategic Design*.

Bent Flyvbjerg is a professor emeritus at the University of Oxford's Saïd Business School. He is a senior research fellow of St. Anne's College at the University of Oxford and the Villum Kann Rasmussen Professor and Chair in Major Program Management at the IT University of Copenhagen.

Vijay Govindarajan is the Coxe Distinguished Professor at Dartmouth College's Tuck School of Business, a Dartmouth-wide chair and the highest distinction awarded to Dartmouth faculty; a faculty partner in the Silicon Valley incubator Mach49; and senior adviser at the strategy consulting firm Acropolis Advisors. He is the *New York Times* and *Wall Street Journal* bestselling author of *Reverse Innovation* and coauthor of *Global by Design: How to Create Innovations That Scale, Travel, and Transform* (Harvard Business Review Press, 2026). Follow him on LinkedIn @vg-govindarajan.

Ruobing Han is an assistant professor at the Chinese University of Hong Kong, Shenzhen, and a recent graduate of Stanford's PhD program in economics, specializing in quantitative marketing. His intellectual curiosity extends to industrial organization and applied microeconomics and the dynamics of the Chinese economy. In addition to his academic pursuits, Ruobing is an avid reader and enjoys playing basketball in his spare time.

Thomas Keil is a professor and the chair in international management at the University of Zurich, Switzerland. He is a partner at The Next Advisors and the coauthor, with Marianna Zangrillo, of *The Next Board: Delivering Value Today While Making the Board Fit for Tomorrow.*

James Liang is a leading scholar of demographic economics, entrepreneurship, and innovation research. He cofounded Trip .com Group and currently serves as its executive chairman. He is also a research professor of applied economics at Peking University's Guanghua School of Management.

Erin Meyer is a professor at INSEAD, where she directs the executive education program Leading Across Borders and Cultures. She is the author of *The Culture Map: Breaking Through the Invisible Boundaries of Global Business* and coauthor (with Reed Hastings) of *No Rules Rules: Netflix and the Culture of Reinvention*.

Paul Swartz is an executive director and senior economist in the BCG Henderson Institute, based in BCG's New York office. He is a coauthor of *Shocks, Crises, and False Alarms: How to Assess True Macroeconomic Risk* (Harvard Business Review Press, 2024).

Melody Wilding is an executive coach, a human behavior professor, and the author of *Managing Up: How to Get What You Need from the People in Charge*. Download exact scripts to diplomatically say no at work at melodywilding.com.

Marianna Zangrillo is a partner at the Next Advisors.

Lily Zheng is a strategist, consultant, and author who works with leaders to build fair, accessible, inclusive, and representative organizations. They are the author of the forthcoming *Fixing Fairness: 4 Tenets to Transform Diversity Backlash into Progress for All*.

M. Zottoli is a statistician in the department of statistics at the University of Oxford.

Index